A Felt Farm

Rotraud Reinhard

A Felt Farm

Floris Books

Translated by Anna Cardwell
Photographs by Jürgen Pfeiffer

First published in German under the title
Auf dem Bauernhof, Filzen für die ganze Familie
by Verlag Freies Geistesleben, Stuttgart
This edition published by Floris Books in 2011

British Library CIP Data available
ISBN 978-086315-789-9
Printed in China

Contents

Introduction: how to use this book

This book has two parts. In the first part are instructions for making a range of felted animals, people and objects for a farm, as well as the farmyard itself. You might want to make just one or two items: a felted child for a doll's house perhaps, or some felted animals to go along with some wooden farm animals you already have. It's quite simple to felt a meadow and a lake for use as a play mat.

The second part of the book is an illustrated story: a day on a farm. In the story, you will see lots of the characters and settings that you've made in the first part. If you prefer, you can use this book solely as a picture book (although a hand-felted cat sitting beside you while you read will strengthen a child's connection to the story).

Making an entire farm is a project for the whole family. Younger ones can try their hand at making apples, balls, puddles and little blankets, and older children can felt simple animals. Parents and other experienced adults can felt the more intricate animals and put the farm structure together. Everyone can add greenery and decorate the farm. A felt farm project is a wonderful way for families to spend time together, working with a common purpose.

Getting Ready for Felting

Tips for felting — read this first!

Choosing materials

- Always use wool batting as the basis of shaped objects. Any wool, coarse or fine, can be used that felts well. However, for miniature animals and for adding colour accents, use only very fine merino wool. For larger animals and figures, merino or regular sheep's wool are both fine. Coarser mountain sheep's wool is better for larger and solid objects, such as houses.
- Washed, uncombed tufts of wool are suitable for paths and the ground. Use coloured curly wool for flowers, plants and other decoration. Coloured wool-silk blends are good for smooth, shiny surfaces like feathers or flowers.
- You'll need soapy water to work. Dissolve the soap in one litre of warm water (soft soap: 1 level tablespoon to 1 litre of hard water).

Shaping objects

- While constructing the objects, the basic shape will still be relatively soft and will not necessarily match your idea of the finished product.
- Always add dry, not wet, tufts of wool to the object and then press them in place with soapy water.
- Once the basic shape is finished, you can felt on additional pieces. Initially, the actual shape is not too important; it's more important to make sure the surface is a solid mass and is well connected to the layer below. Gently vibrate the felt with your whole palm, without pressure.
- Do not rub at the start as this will displace the surface wool layers. If the object feels dry and the wool fibres are standing up, add more water and then put more soap in your hands. If there are too many soap suds, dilute with hot water (use a water sprayer).
- The final shape of the object is only made when you *full* it, towards the end of the process. *Fulling* an object is when you repeatedly press the whole object towards the centre, shaping and thickening in alternation. To full, press, rub, roll, knock and push towards the centre or pull bits longer or thinner. The entire animal will shrink by about a third.
- *After felting you must rinse the soap out thoroughly* (see page 79).
- If you want a combination of two or more colours, tease small tufts of wool together. Place the teased pieces over each other and then tease them apart again. Repeat until you have the desired effect.
- You can cut too long or broad ears into shape after felting. An overly long leg or too fat body part can also be trimmed into shape.

Project times

The small objects described in the first chapter, Simple Projects for Children and Beginners, all take about 15 to 30 minutes to make. The Simple Animals will take 1 to 3 hours. The animals and figures in Intricate Projects for Experienced

Felters will take 3 to 5 hours.

Remember that you can stop the felting process at any time for a break. Place the felted object onto a towel to dry. If it is already well felted, rinse thoroughly and then dry on a towel. Use fresh soapy water when you continue working.

Project materials

wool batt:
beige mountain sheep's wool
white, beige, light brown, medium brown, dark brown, grey merino wool
different colours of dyed merino wool
different brown and beige curly wool for hair and fur (washed, but not carded)

tray, or baking tray, towel, bowl, whisk
soft soap or olive soap, warm water
scissors, ruler, wire cutters
copper wire $1/100$, $3/100$ or $1/16$ in (0.5, 0.8 or 1.5 mm)
fine and medium felting needles
plastic sheet (or garbage bag), bubble wrap
solid plastic templates, small cardboard boxes, cling film (plastic wrap), adhesive tape, thin, bendable twigs, small fur brush (optional)

to embroider: cotton darning thread or embroidery thread, embroidery needle, thin waterproof felt pen, darning needle, 4 wooden buttons

Many of the materials can be obtained from specialist craft shops. See the Resources section at the back of this book for details.

Simple Projects for Children and Beginners

Ball or apple

These are suitable for very young children to make.

MATERIALS
starting piece: 3 $^{1}/_{8}$ x 4 $^{3}/_{4}$ in (8 x 12 cm) or
    1 $^{1}/_{4}$ x 3 $^{1}/_{2}$ in (3 x 9 cm)
$^{1}/_{8}$ oz (3 g) coloured merino wool

Wind up the starting piece tightly, wet and add two tufts of wool at right angles to the layer below. Add extra colours as desired and roll it all carefully between your palms. Once the ball is more solid, press and roll more vigorously. An egg shape can be easily shaped into a ball.

Puddle or small blanket

These are also suitable for very young children.

MATERIALS
starting piece: 4 x 2 $^{3}/_{8}$ in (10 x 6 cm) or 2 $^{3}/_{4}$ x
    2 in (7 x 5 cm)
$^{1}/_{6}$ oz (4 g) coloured merino wool
$^{1}/_{8}$ oz (3 g) brown or blue sheep's wool

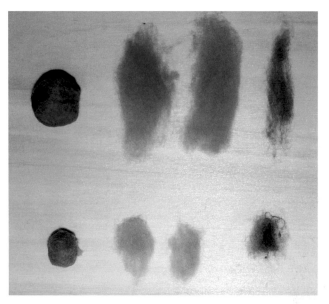

Starting piece with additional wool pieces

Arrange the colours or patterns as desired onto the starting piece and felt in place using a small plastic bag or your palm. Take it between your palms and rub initially gently, then more vigorously. Press and squeeze in different directions until the piece becomes more solid. Straighten the edges by pulling any dents outwards and rubbing bulges towards the centre.

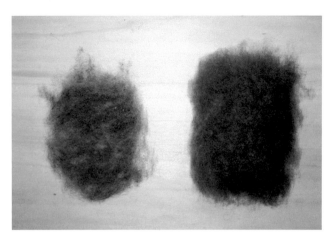
Wool batt

Meadow landscape

MATERIALS

starting piece: 40 x 28 in (100 x 70 cm)
5 1/2 oz (160 g) green wool, optionally with
   flecks of colour or mottled
1 oz (30 g) green and yellow curly wool
44 x 32 in (110 x 80 cm) bubble wrap

Carefully unroll the green wool batt. Separate off one layer and place it onto a slightly larger piece of bubble wrap. Add teased curly wool for flowers and greenery. Using a water sprayer, wet thoroughly with soapy water, press down with a piece of plastic or your flat hands and felt in place by vibrating on the spot without pressure.

Turn the entire piece of wool over including the bubble wrap — either with the help of somebody else or roll it up first — then felt in the same way, counting to 30. To full, roll up the wool with the bubble wrap and gently roll back and forth without pressure. Repeat from all eight sides

(turn it over again). Once the meadow piece has shrunk slightly, repeat the process using a damp towel, this time roll back and forth with pressure, counting to 20. Once the piece feels solid and has shrunk by at least a third, roll and rub the edges inwards to felt completely (felting board). It does not matter if the piece of meadow takes on its own individual shape.

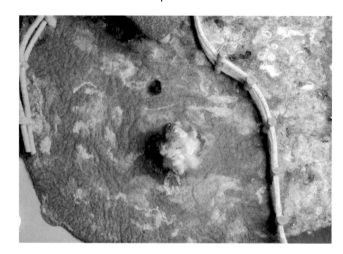

Lake landscape

MATERIALS

starting piece: 24 x 24 in (60 x 60 cm)
3 1/4 oz (90 g) blue merino wool
1 1/2 oz (40 g) green wool batt
1 oz (30 g) different coloured curly wool
28 x 28 in (70 x 70 cm) bubble wrap

Carefully unroll the blue wool batt. Take off one layer of fleece and tease some wool from the corners to make it rounder. Put the wool onto

Fir tree

MATERIALS

starting piece: 8 x 12 in (20 x 30 cm)
1 oz (30 g) brown mountain sheep's wool
2/3 oz (20 g) green curly wool

the bubble wrap. Place green wool around the edges; add coloured curly wool over the green for flowers and greenery. Spread blue, white or green fluffs of wool over the blue to make waves, algae or water lilies.

Using a water sprayer, wet thoroughly with soapy water, press down with the palms of your hand, or with a piece of plastic foil and felt by vibrating. Make sure the whole area is wet through. Turn over carefully with the bubble wrap, and then felt the other side in the same way.

Once the surface has felted well (check that the colours cannot be moved or lifted off), roll up in the bubble wrap. Roll back and forth without pressure, counting to 30 slowly. Repeat this process from each direction and also the other side.

Afterwards, roll up in a damp towel and roll back and forth from each side using pressure, counting to 20. Once the lake has shrunk by at least a third, rub and roll the edges inwards to finish felting them.

Roll up the starting piece from the shorter side and immerse in warm soapy water. Place a few large pieces of curly wool around the lower half to make a cone shape. The lower circumference should be at least 2 3/4 in (7 cm). Roll gently with your flat hand and not much pressure. Gradually rub more vigorously and repeatedly knock the base against the table; full from the tip to the base in your hand or a towel. Press a hollow into the base; this allows the tree to stand securely once dry.

Once the cone is dry, tease the green wool into strands. If the curls are longer than 2 3/4 in (7 cm), cut them in half. Arrange the 'twigs' around the lower part of the cone like a skirt and needle felt the ends in place. Add another skirt further up the cone to cover the base of the first round, needle felt in place in the same way. Continue working upwards until the tree is covered in green. Needle felt the tree top from above. If you want sticking out branches, place a few additional curls at right angles to the tree and needle felt the ends in place at right angles to the cone. This makes the curls stick out.

VARIATION

Add the green curly wool skirt to the base before felting the brown cone. Then felt. This makes a more stable fir tree that is suitable for playing.

Bush or hedge

MATERIALS

2/3 to 1 oz (20 to 30 g) green curly wool or wool matting
thin birch or corkscrew willow twigs

Starting piece, starting roll, finished felt

Twisted twigs, wound with curly wool

16

Wind a round ball, 4 x 4 in (10 x 10 cm) out of bendable twigs or a long garland 16 x 24 in (40 x 60 cm). Wind curly wool randomly around it in two thin layers. The wool need not cover the entire ball evenly. Do not wind too thickly or the structure of the twigs will be hidden.

Felt everything. While fulling, press some areas deeply inwards, but overall do not full too vigorously.

Tree with wire frame

MATERIALS

12 pieces of $3/100$ in (0.8 mm) copper wire, about 35 in (88 cm) long

several 1 1/2 in (4 cm) wide, long strands of wool

5 1/2 oz (160 g) brown mountain sheep's wool

1 1/2 oz (40 g) green curly wool

Twisted wire branches

Twist the 12 pieces of wire together, not quite in the centre (see image above). Divide the shorter ends into 5 to 7 roots, twist some wires double and then further divide them into smaller roots. Divide the longer ends into branches; further

Wind with wool and felt, needle felt curly wool foliage

17

divide the branches to make twigs. Wind long, thin strands of wool batt around it all.

Make the trunk slightly thicker at the base by adding pieces of wool and felting. Roll between your hands and rub on a towel or bubble wrap. Once it has nearly felted, cut a knothole into the trunk. Do not cut too deep or you will expose the wire framework. Re-felt the cut edges.

Once dry, needle felt the leaves in place with green curly wool.

VARIATION

Use rust-coloured and yellow curly wool for an autumn tree, or white for winter.

Feeding trough or sink, or small trough or feeding bowl

MATERIALS

1/2 oz (15 g) brown merino wool or mountain
    sheep's wool
1/4 oz (6 g) white merino wool for the sink
cling film (plastic wrap)
adhesive tape

Feeding trough or sink:
cardboard box, 5 x 1 1/2 x 2 in (13 x 4 x 5 cm)
    or 3 1/8 x 2 3/8 x 1 1/12 in (8 x 6 x 4 cm)

Small trough or feeding bowl:
plastic template, 2 x 1 1/2 in (5 x 4 cm) or 1 1/4
    x 1 1/4 in (3 x 3 cm)

Starting pieces for the feeding trough or sink: Separate off strands of wool batting slightly narrower than the box's width and double the length of the box's circumference.

First wind cling film (plastic wrap) around the whole box and stick the ends in place with adhesive tape to make it waterproof. Wind the starting piece strand firmly around the cardboard box, repeat with a second strand winding in the other direction to completely cover the box. Wet well each time. Add more wool to the corners and any thin areas. Once the surface is lightly felted, rub the wool well against the cardboard.

To make a **feeding trough or deep sink**, cut around the upper edge of the felted box at the desired height. Cutting around the centre of the box makes two shallow troughs. Remove the box to full the troughs. Fold the narrow sides inwards to keep corners and edges sharp.

Make **small troughs and feeding bowls** using a plastic template. Place pieces of wool over one side of the template, wet well, turn the template around, smooth the overhanging ends of wool around the edges. Add the remaining three pieces of wool over this side of the template in the same way. Cut open along the top edge and remove the template. Push the base downwards and smooth everything into place well while fulling.

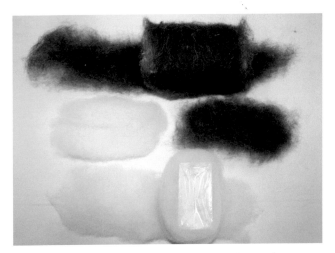

Wind around the box in one direction, place a layer over it crosswise

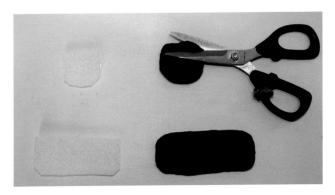

Template, felted, before cutting open

Rabbit hutch

MATERIALS

starting piece: strands of wool, 3 1/8 in (8 cm) wide, approximately double the length of the box's circumference

1/2 oz (11 g) fine to medium brown and mottled grey merino/sheep's wool

fly swatter or fine meshed wire

small cardboard box, approximately 3 1/2 x 2 x 2 1/2 in (9 x 5 x 6 cm)

cling film (plastic wrap)

adhesive tape

Wrap cling film (plastic wrap) around the cardboard box and stick adhesive tape to the edges to make it completely waterproof. Using thin strands, wind wool firmly around the box twice in one direction, twice in the other direction to cover the box entirely with wool. Place additional pieces of wool over the corners and any thin areas. Once the surface is felted, rub well against the box.

For the lid, cut around three sides of the upper edge, leaving the back, longer edge uncut. Place grey mottled wool over both sides of the lid, smooth the overhanging wool over the edges, making the lid larger than the hutch. Carefully felt the grey wool in place.

Remove the cardboard box; fold the hutch flat so it can be rolled up. Full the sides slanting downwards slightly and the front shorter so that the roof slopes downwards when shut. After fulling, cut a rectangle out of the front and re-felt these edges. Once dry, sew fly or wire netting to the hole on the inside.

VARIATION: HEN HOUSE OR SHED

Felt around a larger cardboard box. After fulling, cut out a door and one or two windows.

1. *Place the box, wound once, on the wool batt*
2. *Wrap up well*

Cut open the lid

Place wool on the lid, second lid piece

Full by rolling

Fold together to continue fulling

Once fulled, cut a rectangle out of the front

Tables and benches

starting pieces: 12 x 12 in (30 x 30 cm) or 11 x 11 in (28 x 28 cm)
3 oz (90 g) beige and dark brown merino/sheep's wool

Place a smaller dark brown piece of wool over the beige wool. Roll up tightly from the narrow side; a second person can be a great help. Immerse the roll in soapy water and gently roll. Gradually increase pressure, pushing the ends towards the centre. To finish, roll up in a wet towel and roll vigorously.

Cut off the ends with a sharp knife. You need to cut 4 equal-size and 2 thicker slabs off both ends. Cut the remaining centre piece, approximately 4 3/4 to 5 in (12 to 13 cm) long and 2 in (5 cm) thick, into three pieces lengthwise (see image bottom right). The central piece is the table top, the outside pieces the benches. Once they are rinsed and dried, place two discs each under the table top and benches and sew or glue in place (you could use a hot glue gun).

Roll up tightly

VARIATION

A roll just under 1 1/4 in (3 cm) thick and 4 3/4 in (12 cm) long will make 2 small benches. You can make a large oval table top by placing two oval pieces of wool batt 5 3/4 x 4 in (15 x 10 cm) on top of each other. Fold back the edges and felt and full well.

You can also use a bench piece for the kitchen counter. Use a leftover piece of roof (see page 91) for the cupboard below. Add the wooden counter and the sink to the top of the cupboard once they are dry and sew or glue in place (you could use a hot glue gun).

Cut the bench board

Ring cake or bread

MATERIALS
starting piece: 3 1/4 x 2 in (8 x 5 cm)
1/32 to 1/16 oz (1 to 2 g) light, medium and dark brown merino/sheep's wool

Roll a solid round or oval shape, pushing the edges inwards repeatedly, and immerse in soapy water. Place at least two pieces of wool at right angles to the layer below and add more wool until the bread is the desired size. To make a ring cake, add lighter and darker wool as a last layer. Optionally, decorate the bread with 'flour' or 'seeds.' Felt in place while rolling. Only felt the final ring cake shape when fulling. Felt the base flat and press a hole into the top with a pair of scissors. Make the grooves by repeatedly squeezing the top together between thumb and forefinger. Press the bread flat and cut slanting ridges into the top with a sharp knife to finish.

Starting roll and further wool pieces for the ring cake or bread

Pillow

MATERIALS

starting piece: 3 1/4 x 3 1/4 in (8 x 8 cm)
1/6 oz (4 g) mottled merino wool

Fold in all four sides to make a 1 1/2 in (4 cm) large square. Wind two approximately 4 in (10 cm) long strands from each side around the pillow. This ensures the centre is thicker than the edges. After initial felting, press the corners together slightly and in between stroke towards the centre.

Doll's pram

MATERIALS

starting pieces: 3 1/2 x 1 1/2 in (9 x 4 cm) (2
    pieces)
handle: 3/4 x 3 1/4 in (2 x 8 cm)
2 to 2 3/4 in (5 to 7 cm) long egg-shape template
4 wooden buttons
1/4 oz (7 g) red-brown mottled merino wool

Wind wool strands firmly around the egg template from all directions, wet thoroughly and press down well. Apply a further three thin layers, gently felt on, then full very vigorously. Cut a third out of the top for the pram blanket with a pair of sharp scissors. Remove the template.

Use a thin wool strand for the handle and needle felt it firmly in place, felt it on well while fulling the whole pram (if necessary, sew in place). Sew on the four buttons for wheels once dry.

Egg template on the starting piece, further pieces of wool needed, handle

Cut out the top, needle felt handle in place

Doll or baby

MATERIALS

1/100 in (0.5 mm) copper wire, 2 3/8 in (6 cm) long

head: 3/16 x 1 1/2 in (0.5 x 4 cm)

body: 3/8 x 3/4 in (1 x 2 cm) (2 pieces)

1/32 oz (1 g) white, skin-colour, yellow-brown, and pink merino wool

Twist a small loop, about 1/5 in (0.5 cm), into the centre of the wire. Pull the white strand of wool approximately 3/4 in (2 cm) through it and wind it firmly around the head loop. Do not wind a neck or a connection to the shoulder. Wind skin-colour wool around the entire head, which should be approximately 3/8 in (1 cm) wide.

For the **hands**, wind two 1/8 x 5/8 in (0.3 x 1.5 cm) long strands of skin-colour wool around the end of the arm wires and fold back the wire about 3/16 in (0.5 cm) — this means there is already some wool around the bend and the wool cannot slip. Wind the remaining wool around this loop to make the hand. If you can still feel the wire through the wool, wind an additional layer of wool around it.

Pull the pink **body** wool apart slightly at the top and tease the ends thinner. Place the thin ends over the shoulders just beside the head; fold back at the base so that the body appears to be too short. Add a second body piece in the same way from the other side. Pad out the body with one or two pieces of wool. Wind thinly around the arms with a narrow wool strand, covering the base of the hand. Connect the body to the arms with two to three tiny layers at the shoulders and armpits.

Place a thin yellow-brown piece of wool onto the head for **hair**. Alternatively, to make a hat, fold back the front edge of a thin strip of pink wool, place it over the head leaving the face free, and overlap the ends at the back of the head. Optionally, add some pieces of wool to make a peak. Mix pink and light pink wool and spread it thinly over the entire hat for the last layer.

After felting, full the body towards the centre. Full the neck above the shoulders. Felt the face and hat or hair separately so the edge of the hat or hair is still clearly visible. Full a faint eye line into the centre of the face with your fingernails. Full the arms in place at the sides, do not push them up or away from the body.

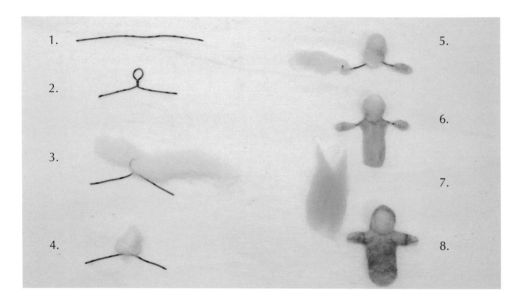

1. Piece of wire
2. Twisted loop for head
3. Pull starting piece 3/4 in (2 cm) through the head loop
4. Wind white wool around the head
5. Wind skin-colour wool around the head, wind 3/16 in (0.5 cm) around the end of the wire for hands
6. Place pink body piece over the shoulders and fold back
7. Second body piece
8. Wind body thinly with pink mottled wool, add hair piece to head

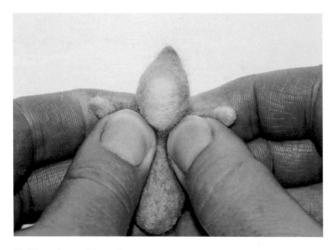

Full neck and head

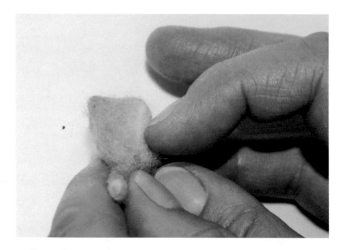

Full eye line

Simple animals

Hen

MATERIALS
starting piece: 2 3/4 x 2 3/4 in (7 x 7 cm)
head: 3/4 x 3/4 in (2 x 2 cm)
1/32 oz (1 g) brown, black rust mottled, red, and
    yellow sheep's wool

Wind a larger and smaller oval roll, immerse both in soapy water, put the smaller oval (the head) onto the larger one (the body) and add a small piece of wool to connect them. Place three to four tiny pieces of wool around the neck. To make a downwards facing head, put the head further forward on the body and pull downwards once connected to the body.

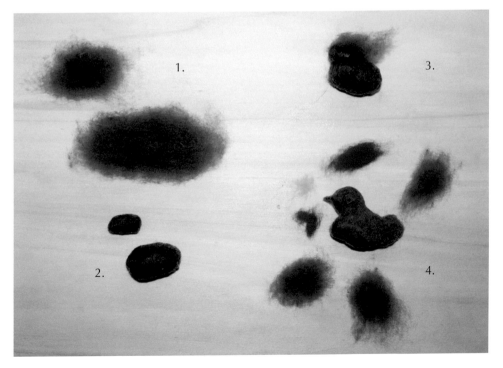

1. Starting pieces
2. Body and head pieces rolled up
3. Wool piece connecting body and head
4. Head and body connected, beak and tail teased out, wool for wattle, beak and further pieces

Pull the tail upwards, tease a tiny beak out of the front or side of the head (the hen then looks sideways). Tease out the comb in the same way. Add yellow and red wool to the beak and comb, needle felt the wattle under the beak with a tiny piece of red wool and cut in two with a pair of scissors. Arrange brown body colour around the head. Build up the chest, centre of the body and tail with a few layers. Place some mottled wool over chest and tail.

After carefully felting it all in place, full towards the body centre and push the wings together. Full the neck slightly and turn, push or pull the head in the desired direction. Cut into the comb twice and re-felt. Shower it ten times and let it dry on a towel (for eyes, see page 78).

Duck

MATERIALS

body: 2 3/4 x 2 3/4 in (7 x 7 cm)
head: 3/4 x 3/4 in (2 x 2 cm)
wings: 1/2 x 1 1/2 in (1.5 x 4 cm) (2 pieces)
1/16 oz (2 g) light brown, dark brown, and
    yellow merino/sheep's wool

Start as for Hen (page 27). After attaching the head to the body, pull out a long neck. Keep the body thin, fill the chest well and make a round head. Cover the fairly broad, long bill with yellow wool and attach well to the head. Cover any yellow on the head with head colour again and add the desired colours to the body. Place a wing at each side and needle felt their bases in place. Shape the ends to a point, fold back and then wet. While fulling, bend the bill upwards slightly and press an edge into the upper side. Make a round head. The head and neck should be shaped like an S.

Full the wings

Nearly-finished duck with mottled wool and bill piece

Bill covered in yellow, wing needle felted in place and shaped to a point

Goose

MATERIALS
body: 3 1/2 x 3 1/2 in (9 x 9 cm)
wings: 1 1/4 x 3/4 in (3 x 2 cm)
1/8 oz (3 g) white, plus some orange, merino/
    sheep's wool

Pull the head with bill out of the rolled–up starting piece. Make the chest and body plump and stumpy. Make the bill wedge-shaped using orange wool, keep the head small and slightly round. Place the wing pieces on both sides, needle felt the bases in place and fold back the tips to make a point. Add two thin wool layers for more stability. While fulling, full a long S shape into the head and neck. Full the body well towards the centre.

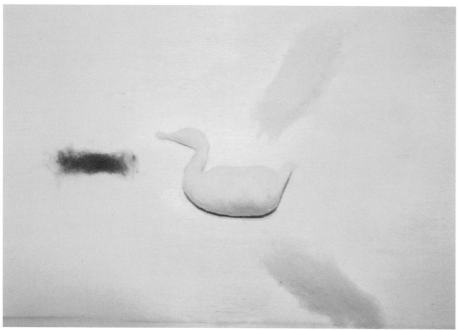

Rolled–up starting piece, head and neck pulled out, wing and beak wool

Rabbit

MATERIALS

body: 3 1/2 x 1 1/4 in (9 x 3 cm)
head: 2 3/8 x 3/4 in (6 x 2 cm)
ears: 2 3/8 x 3/4 in (6 x 2 cm)
1/8 oz (3 g) brown merino wool

Start as for Hen (page 27). Fill chest and body well, adding plenty of wool particularly to the back of the body. Make the head oval. Pull out the tail at the base of the back, add another piece of wool and cover with the desired colour. Arrange the ear piece on the head in an omega shape (Ω), needle felt in place and split into two ears; if necessary, cut them with a pair of scissors. From behind, add two thin wool pieces around both ears and then add one wool piece from the front. Place a thin piece from the back of the head over each ear. The ears should look too large and wide as they shrink considerably while fulling.

After felting, fold them in half lengthways and rub them between your fingers to full them narrow. Full the tip by holding the ear at the back and rubbing from the front. Shape the head in a curve from the ears to the mouth. Shape the body by pushing the tail and front together repeatedly with your thumb and forefinger.

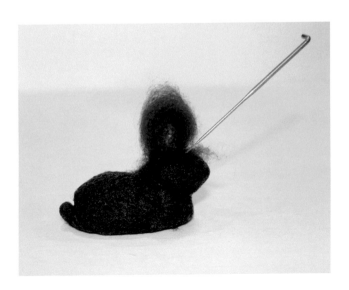

Needle felt the ears in place

Ears split in half

Lamb

MATERIALS
body: 2 3/8 x 1 1/4 in (6 x 3 cm)
1/32 oz (1 g) black merino wool

Pull the thin starting piece slightly longer at the front; this makes a narrow head and neck. Economically add a few pieces of wool at right angles to the layer below. Make the backside slightly wider. Make relatively long ears. Add a thin layer of short curly wool. While fulling, make the forehead round and bend the head to the side or upwards.

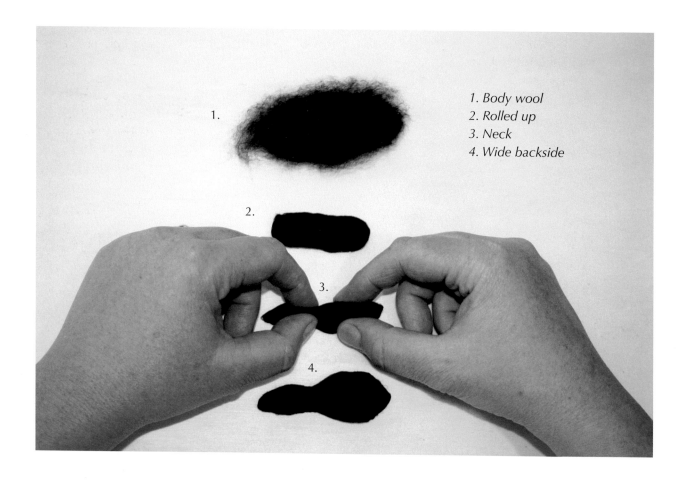

1. Body wool
2. Rolled up
3. Neck
4. Wide backside

Sheep

MATERIALS
body: 5 1/2 x 2 3/4 in (14 x 7 cm)
head: 2 3/8 x 1 1/4 in (6 x 3 cm)
1/8 oz (5 g) white merino wool
1/6 oz (4 g) white curly wool

Start as for Hen (page 27). Make the body plump and round, the head longish. Place floppy ears over the top to the side of the head or make smaller standing ears from the front to the back and attach. Add pieces of wool over the mouth and under the ears. Tease the curly wool slightly and make an oval 'sheepskin.' Put the sheep in the centre of it, and wrap the 'skin' around the body, if necessary needle felt in place. Either leave the head bare, or place a few curls around the forehead.

While fulling, pinch the backside together to hint at a tail. Press the back down with your left or right thumb. This lengthens the body and gives it a slight curve. Once dry, tease out the curls using a sewing needle or needle felt a further layer of curly wool over the sheep.

Add the ears

Sheep placed in the curly wool fleece

Piglet

MATERIALS

body: 2 3/8 x 3/4 in (6 x 2 cm)

1/16 oz (2 g) white and skin-coloured merino
  wool

Add skin-coloured wool to the piglet

Make head and body out of a single white piece. Add pieces of wool to the body to fatten. Place slightly curved ears on top of the head. Build up the head at the sides and top. Needle felt a thin, 3/4 in (2 cm) long, skin-coloured tail in place and add two tiny pieces of wool to connect. Cover well with skin-coloured felt. While fulling make a neck and bend the head upwards. Press around the snout to make it narrower and press against the front of the snout with your thumb to make it round. Needle felt two nose holes and an upwards curving line for the mouth (see page 77).

Intricate Projects for Experienced Felters

Sitting animals

Dog

MATERIALS

body: 2 3/8 x 1 1/4 in (6 x 3 cm)
tail: 2 3/8 x 3/8 in (6 x 1 cm)
legs: 2 3/8 x 3/4 in (6 x 2 cm)
ears: 1 1/2 x 3/8 in (4 x 1 cm) (2 pieces)
1/4 oz (7 g) brown and dark brown, and white
    merino wool

Put the tail piece on the body piece at right angles. Roll the body up tightly and immerse in soapy water. Place the leg in an omega shape (Ω) from front to back onto the centre of the body. Wet the base and separate the legs in two. If necessary, use a pair of scissors to cut right up to the body. Wet everything and add a connecting piece of felt around each leg. Turn the whole body around and continue building up the body. Leave the legs lying stretched forwards. Do not put wool between the tops of the legs.

Starting at the side, place a few strands of wool over the paws and up to the body. Pull out the chest slightly and add a few layers at right angles. Wind thin strands around the head and build up the muzzle by attaching small strands of wool crosswise from the front. Place a few pieces over the body and neck. Add pieces from the side and from below to the bottom and thighs.

Long–haired dogs need to be made fatter and their tail broader. Place the ears over the top of

the head to the sides in an omega shape (Ω). Connect with a few wool pieces and add one or two thin pieces of wool batt to the ears.

Towards the end of constructing the animal, place it on its side and push the legs and bottom together. Add missing wool to the backside from below. Check whether chest and muzzle are large enough. It is better to make it all slightly too fat. Too much mass is easier to shape while fulling than not enough.

Place white pieces of wool on the chest, tapering it over the muzzle to the forehead. Place tiny pieces of dark brown wool at the side of the mouth, if necessary needle felt in place. With your left forefinger and middle finger on the chest and front legs, and the right hand on the back, carefully felt by shaking. Gently press on each leg individually, ears and tail too.

Put the head downwards into your palm and felt, including the ears. Do not hold on to the back of the dog as this needs to be shaped round. While fulling, push the head upwards, work the ears thinner and slightly slanting forwards. Full the tail shorter, flat and slightly bent.

1. Tail wool placed over body piece
2. Starting piece with leg wool
3. Leg wool placed over the centre
4. Legs divided in half, base attached, second wool piece connecting leg
5. Turn over to the stomach
6. Padded out slightly, before adding the ears

Repeatedly push the thighs together by pressing the back and front together using thumb and fore and middle finger. Full the muzzle towards the head by pushing it in a circular motion. Shape it into a triangle slanting slightly upwards. Push the forehead and muzzle together slightly, at the same time fulling the forehead flatter. Shower ten times and let dry on a towel (for eyes, see page 78).

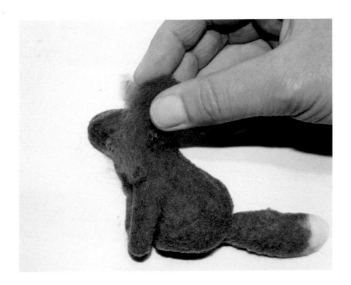

Add the ears in an omega shape (Ω)

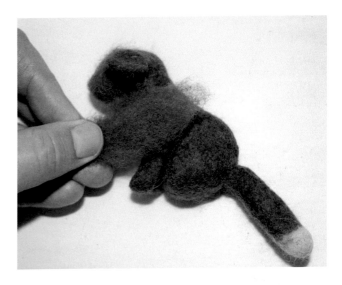

Add the chest wool piece

Place a wool piece from one ear to the other

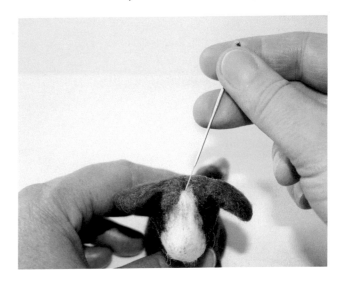

Needle felt white markings in place

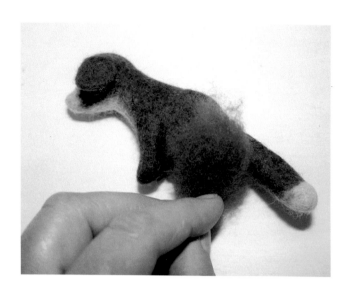

Add thigh wool piece

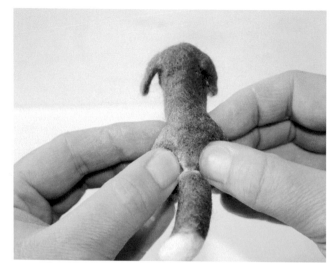

Full thighs

How to hold while felting in place

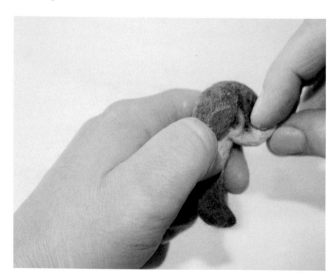

Shape the muzzle

Full towards the centre

Squeeze muzzle and head together

Cat

MATERIALS
body: 3/4 x 3/8 in (2 x 1 cm)
leg: 1 1/4 x 1/2 in (3 x 1.5 cm)
tail: 1 1/4 x 3/16 in (3 x 0.5 cm)
ears: 2/8 x 3/4 in (1 x 2 cm)
1/32 oz (1 g) white, red-brown, dark brown merino wool

Make a small, thin body with narrow legs and tail. Add strands of dark reddish-brown wool. Make the ears stick upwards in a triangular shape and build up a small muzzle. Stretch the neck slightly while fulling. Position the tail around the body or bend it sideways and felt the ears to a point. Optionally, you can full one paw pointing upwards.

VARIATION: LYING DOWN CAT OR DOG
Add less wool at the backside and make the body slightly elongated. While felting and fulling, press your left forefinger between chest and legs and grasp around the body from above. Push the thighs together at the back, and circle around them from the front several times (see image p39 bottom left).

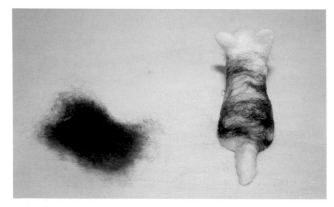

Add the stripes

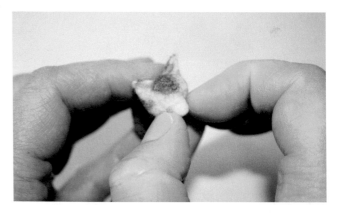

Shape the nose

Rabbit

MATERIALS
body: 1 1/4 x 1 1/4 in (3 x 3 cm)
leg: 1 1/2 x 1/2 in (4 x 1.5 cm)
ears: 2 3/8 x 3/4 in (6 x 2 cm)
1/16 oz (2 g) white and black merino wool

Make relatively broad and long ears (they shrink a lot when fulled). Place two thin layers from the back to the front around both ears to connect them to the head and keep them together. Optionally, add a further piece from the back to the ear. Make the head slightly oval. Add at least two wool pieces across the head in front of the ears. Pull out the tail at the base of the back, add a connecting piece over it and cover with black wool. Full the chest slim and the ears narrow by folding them together and rubbing from the side. To make the ear tips pointed, hold the back of the tips with one hand and rub against it with the other.

VARIATION: LYING DOWN
See dog and cat instructions on page 40.

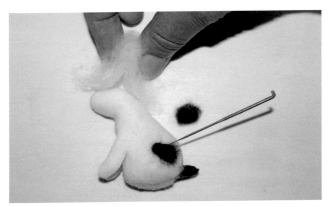

Add the ears, needle felt spots in place

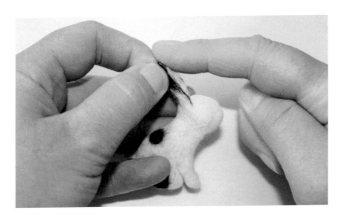

Shape pointed ears

Pig

MATERIALS

body: 1 1/4 x 2 in (3 x 5 cm)
legs: 1 1/4 x 1/2 in (3 x 1.5 cm)
ears: 1 1/4 x 3/8 in (3 x 1 cm) (2 pieces)
tail: 3/16 x 1 1/2 in (0.5 x 4 cm)
1/6 oz (4 g) white and pink merino wool

Make a thick neck. Legs should be short, but not too fat. Fatten the back and thighs well with many layers of wool. Make the ears relatively long and shape them slanting inwards. Place a few layers over the head for the snout. Cover everything with large pieces of pink wool. You should not be able to see any white areas any more. Carefully felt in place. While fulling, repeatedly push well towards the centre so that the pig remains nice and plump. Full the thin legs downwards. Shape a thin and oblong snout by circling and pressing from above. Press the typically flat circle at the front of the snout with your thumb. Needle felt the nose holes and the triangular mouth while still wet (see also page 77).

Standing animals

Pig

Materials

body: 1 1/2 x 1 1/2 in (4 x 4 cm)
legs: 2 x 3/4 in (5 x 2 cm) (2 pieces)
ears: 2 3/4 x 3/8 in (7 x 1 cm) (2 pieces)
tail: 1 1/2 x 3/16 in (4 x 0.5 cm)
1/4 oz (8 g) white, skin-coloured, and optionally brown (for spots) merino wool

Roll up the body starting piece tightly, push in any fibres sticking out the sides. Immerse in soapy water. Arrange the legs lengthways at the centre and back of the body roll in an omega shape, divide into two and press each leg together. Place a small piece of connecting wool at the start of each leg. To continue building up the body, place the body on its side. Make the legs relatively thin and not too short. Hardly put any wool between the legs. Build up the body nice and plump by placing several lengthwise layers on the side and top of it, and also from the back, crosswise over the bottom. Place a few pieces at the side from the bottom to the inside thighs (backside).

Place several layers lengthwise and crosswise over the head. Before it is finished, add the ears one at a time in an omega shape, slightly to the sides. Shape them slanting towards the centre of the head.

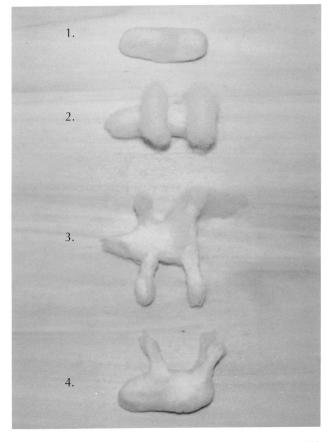

1. Starting roll
2. Add legs
3. Separate legs, wool piece connecting them to body
4. Place on its side

Enlarge the snout with a few crosswise layers. Check if everything looks round and plump and if necessary add more layers. Fasten or needle felt the tail in place using skin-coloured wool and two to three connecting pieces, at the same time covering the backside with skin-coloured wool. Completely cover the back with a large piece of skin-coloured wool, and place separate smaller pieces around ears and legs. Wind firmly around the legs, but not too thickly.

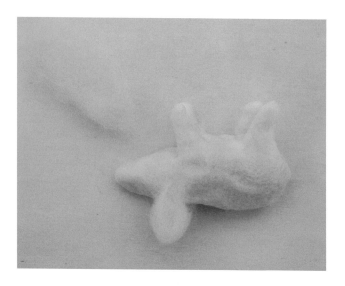

Ear added, second ear wool piece

Attach the ear from the back to the front

Needle felt the tail in place

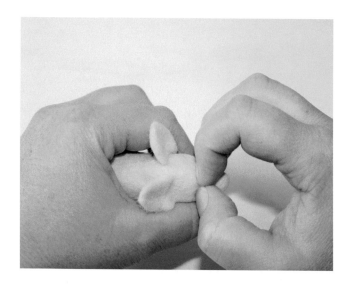

Shape the snout

Carefully felt in place. Shape the backside and back round, full the legs thin, do not full much of a neck or chest. Press the thighs inwards slightly and hint at the backside crack. Shape the ears first thinner and then slightly pointy, then bend them forwards and press a slight edge in the centre. Full the snout by pressing in a circular motion from above. Press against the snout with your thumb to make it round. Needle felt the nose holes and mouth line while still wet (see page 77). Shower ten times and let it dry on a towel (for eyes, see page 78).

Shape a round mouth

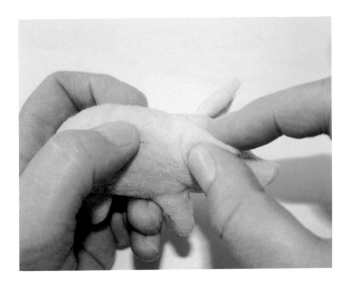

Shape the ears

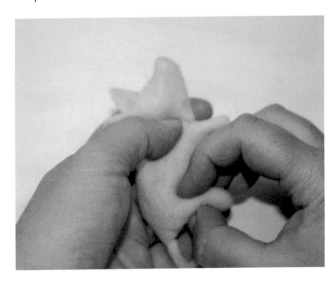

Full the thighs, bend the head to the side

Dog

MATERIALS
body: 1 1/2 x 2 3/8 in (4 x 6 cm)
tail: 1/2 x 2 in (1.5 x 5 cm)
legs: 3/4 x 2 in (2 x 5 cm) (2 pieces)
ears: 3/8 x 2 in (1 x 5 cm) (2 pieces)
1/3 oz (9 g) brown, dark brown, white merino/
    sheep's wool

Roll the tail into the body piece. Fatten the body
into a rectangular shape, make the legs relatively
long. Furry dogs need to be made fatter than
short-haired dogs. Add on floppy ears, and then
build up the head lengthwise and crosswise
below the ears. Do not forget the backside and
thighs. Needle felt the coat colours and patterns.
Hold the dog in one hand, two fingers between
the legs and your forefinger in front of the chest,
and then gently shake it with the other hand
to felt everything in place. During this process
lengthen the body and develop the head and
neck. Full the snout gently, circling from above,
and shape a triangle at the front. Bend the tail
upwards slightly.

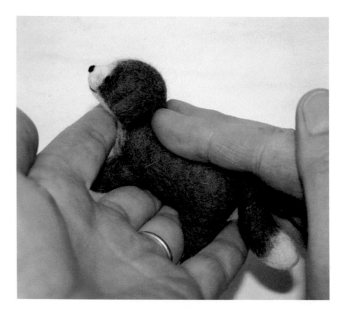

Full the legs apart, stretch the body

Cat

MATERIALS

body: 1 $^1/_4$ x $^3/_4$ in (3 x 2 cm)
tail: 1 $^1/_4$ x $^3/_{16}$ in (3 x 0.5 cm)
legs: $^3/_8$ x 1 $^1/_4$ in (1 x 3 cm) (2 pieces)
ears: $^3/_8$ x $^3/_4$ in (1 x 2 cm)
$^1/_{16}$ oz (1.5 g) white, orange, brown merino/
    sheep's wool

Make the cat thin using small pieces of wool. Do not make the tail too short. Make the body rectangular. Add the ears before the head is too large. Fill the cheeks below the ears. Hold the cat with one finger on the stomach and two on the back to felt everything in place. Make the ears nicely pointed and, if desired, full the legs into a walking position.

Lamb or kid

MATERIALS
body: 3/4 x 1 1/4 in (2 x 3 cm)
legs: 1/2 x 1 1/2 in (1.5 x 4 cm) (2 pieces)
ears: 3/16 x 3/4 in (0.5 x 2 cm) (2 pieces)
tail: 3/16 x 1 1/2 in (0.5 x 4 cm)
1/16 oz (2 g) white, brown merino wool

Make long thin legs. Use a few thin pieces of wool to build up. Make the forehead round, the backside somewhat fatter. Place a thin layer of fine curly wool over the lamb's body. Full the neck bending slightly forward. Full the forehead round and bend the muzzle upwards slightly. Shape the tail sideways as if wagging.

Before adding the ears

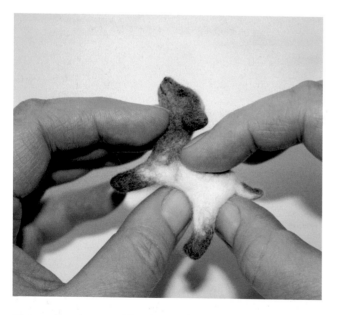

Shape the chest and back curved

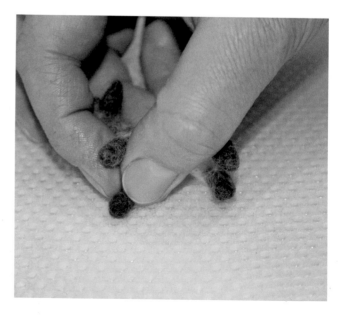

Full the legs thin and firm

48

Poultry with wire legs

Rooster

MATERIALS

legs: $1/100$ in (0.5 mm) copper wire, 13 $1/2$ in
   (34 cm) long
body: $3/4$ x 2 $3/4$ in (2 x 7 cm)
tail feathers: 2 $3/4$ x 3 $1/2$ in (7 x 9 cm)
$1/6$ oz (5 g) brown, red, beige, yellow merino
   wool
blue-green and rust-coloured wool-silk roving

Bend the wire in half, twist four claws on each
side about 1 $1/2$ in (4 cm) from the middle of the
wire, then twist the ends back up to the bend.
Wind beige wool thinly around the wire until it
is covered, and felt in place. If this process seems
too complicated, you can leave the wire legs
bare.

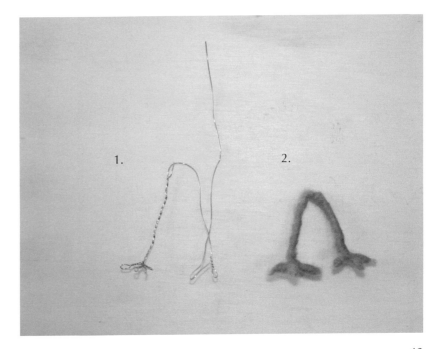

1. Wind the claws
out of wire
2. Wind wool thinly
around the claws

Push the body starting piece between the legs in a V shape and wind a piece of wool around it at right angles. Place pieces of wool lengthwise and crosswise over chest and tail. Pull a tuft of wool out of the head for the beak and add one or two tiny pieces of wool to it. Add the comb from the side up to the top of the head. Wind yellow wool around the beak, needle felt two red wattles under each side of the beak. Then cover head, chest and body with brown wool.

Cut some rust-coloured wool-silk roving into 3/4 in (2 cm) short pieces, arrange over head and chest. Cut the thin fibres off one side of the green-blue wool-silk roving tail. Divide the cut side into 13 strands for approximately two thirds of the length. Felt the single strands, but not the connected end piece. Wind this end around the back of the rooster's body and connect using two thin layers of brown wool. Add a blue-green spot for feathers at the top of the wings. Fold short, rust-coloured wool-silk fibres in half and add these 'feathers' over the sides and tail base. Carefully felt in place, then full the body in a V shape; bend the head forwards and fan out the tail feathers. Full the beak thin, pointy and slightly curved.

Body wool in a V shape

Body slightly built up

Comb and wattles in place, tail piece

Partially-felted tail piece placed on the body

Add feathers

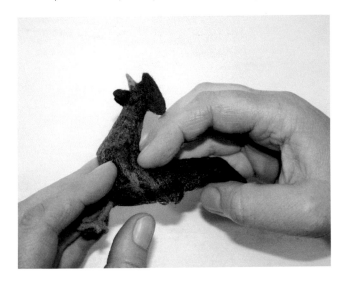

Full a V shape and thin chest

Cut into comb

Hen

MATERIALS

legs: $^1/_{100}$ in (0.5 mm) copper wire, 12 $^1/_2$ in
(32 cm) long

body: $^3/_4$ x 2 in (2 x 5 cm)

$^1/_{16}$ oz (2 g) white, beige, brown, red, yellow
merino wool

Make the hen shorter and fatter than the rooster.
Make the tail short and the body rounder. The
comb and wattles should be smaller than the
rooster's.

Goose

MATERIALS

legs: $1/100$ in (0.5 mm) copper wire, 12 in (30 cm) long

body: $2 \, 3/8 \times 1 \, 1/4$ in (6 x 3 cm)

wings: $2 \times 3/4$ in (5 x 2 cm) (2 pieces)

$1/8$ oz (3 g) white, orange merino wool

Make the feet webbed, rather than with individual claws. Wind orange wool around the legs. Push the body piece between the legs, pull the head upwards and the tail straight back. Add lots of layers to make the body fat. Make the bill relatively large and wedge-shaped; make a round head and a plump breast. Arrange the wings at the sides. Needle felt the bases of the wings in place and fold the tips back into a point. While fulling, make the head and neck into an S shape. Full a sharp edge along the top of the bill.

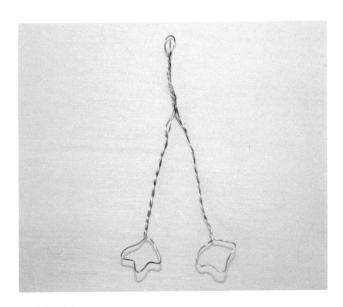

Webbed feet

Standing animals with wire legs

Cow

MATERIALS

legs: $3/100$ in (0.8 mm) copper wire, 2 pieces
    each 8 $1/4$ in (21 cm) long
head/neck: 7 x 1 $1/2$ in (18 x 4 cm)
ears: 2 $3/4$ x $3/4$ in (7 x 2 cm) (2 pieces)
horns: 2 $3/4$ x $1/2$ in (7 x 1.5 cm)
udder: $3/8$ x 3 $1/2$ in (1 x 9 cm)
teats: $3/8$ x 1 in (1 x 2.5 cm) (2 pieces)
tail: 8 $1/2$ in (22 cm)
1 oz (30 g) white, brown, beige and skin-
    coloured merino/sheep's wool
brown tiny curled wool

Twist the two pieces of wire together several times
for about 1 $1/4$ in (3 cm), not quite in the centre:
the back legs should be at least $1/2$ in (1.5 cm)
longer than the front legs. Wind a thin strand of
wool around each of the wire ends several times,
bend back the wire $1/16$ in (0.5 cm) and wind
wool around them again. Wind thinly and evenly
up to the top of the legs. Wind at least $3/4$ in (2
cm) around the centre of the body. Add pieces of
wool to the left and right side for the chest and
head. Pull the chest out towards the front and pre-
shape the head.

    Wet it all well. Place a lot of layers over the
chest, stomach, back, backside, back thighs,

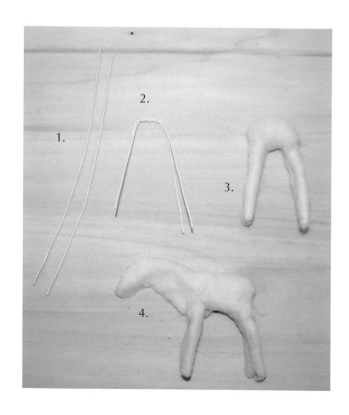

1. Wire pieces
2. Leg frame
3. Wind thinly around legs and body
4. Body chest wool added

shoulders, neck and head. Place a few layers lengthwise over the back. At the sides, place separate layers over the shoulders, stomach and thighs. Add more wool to the legs and wind beige wool thinly around the hooves.

Add the **ears** at the sides while the head still looks too small, from front to back in an omega shape (Ω). They should appear too large. Connect with a piece of wool placed from the back to the front. Needle felt the thin horns to the head

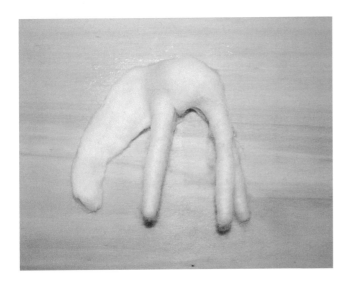

Head and chest wool for a grazing cow

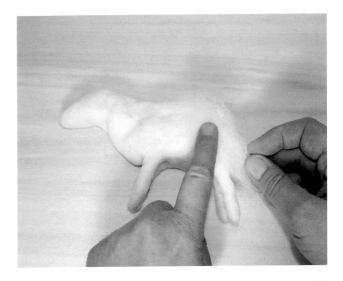

Build up the thighs

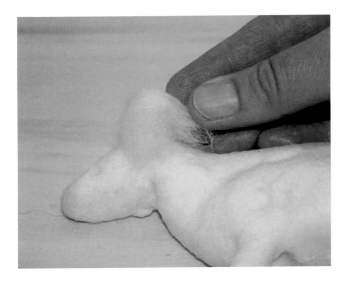

Add the ear

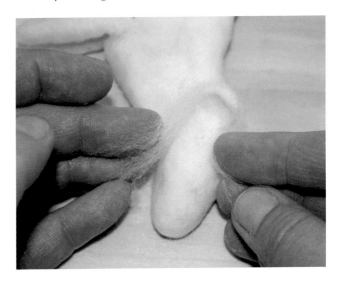

Attach the ear from the back to the front

between the ears. Attach to the head with three or four layers of wool. Add beige wool to the horns until they are the correct size. Place 2 to 3 thin pieces of wool over the whole ear, alternating from the front and back. Place several layers lengthwise and crosswise over the head.

Attach the long **tail** to the top of the backside and add sufficient wool to the sides. Make the tail thicker at the base. Wind a small wool oval, approximately 1/2 in (1.5 cm) circumference, for the

Needle felt horns in place

Attach the horns

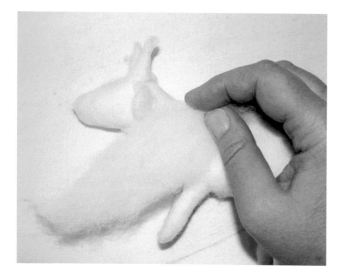

Build up the chest

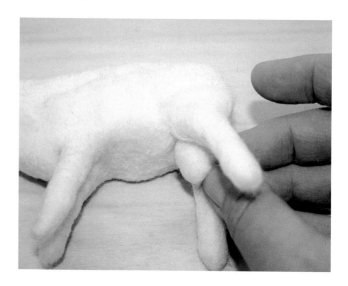

Add the udder

udder, place it between the back legs, cover with a piece of wool and add several pieces around it to attach it. Add the two skin-coloured teat pieces, needle felt them in place and split each one in two. Place a piece of wool around each teat to connect and cover the entire udder with skin-coloured wool. Make sure the udder with teats is not too large. Check whether the stomach and thighs are fat enough.

Add the distinctive cow markings with brown

Needle felt the teats in place

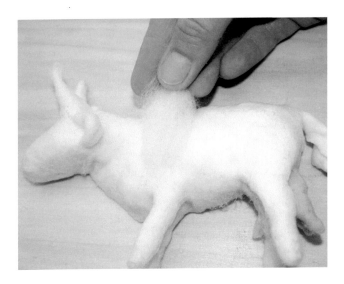

Build up the shoulder

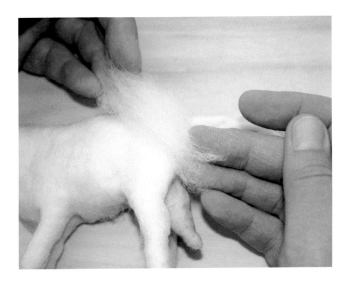

Build up backside and back

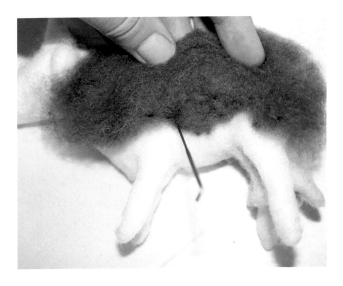

Needle felt hide markings

wool and needle felt the edges in place. Add a thin layer of white wool over the remaining white areas. Place some skin-coloured wool over the mouth.

As the legs do not shrink lengthwise while fulling, at this stage the whole body should appear too large and the legs too short in relation. Full the chest tapering towards the front, full a square backside and the stomach behind the shoulders and in front of the thighs. While doing so, pull down the back legs slightly as they usually slip too far into the body. Arrange head, neck and back at the same height and repeatedly push towards the centre. Fold the ears together and rub the sides between your fingers, bend the horns in an upwards curve.

Full the head flatter towards the nose and getting thinner towards the mouth. Press the mouth upwards lightly against the head and full it round. Full the neck thinner at the sides below the head. Needle felt nose holes and mouth line while still wet (see page 77). Rub along the sides of the legs and tail. Shower ten times and let dry on a towel. Once dry, you can sew a few curls between the horns and tail tuft (see also page 79). Either needle felt on the eyes (see page 78) or embroider them (see page 82).

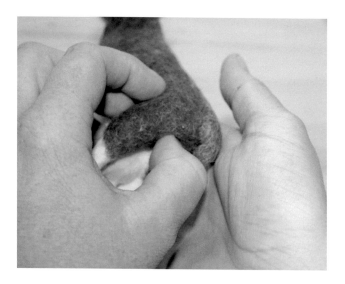

Full the thighs

Full the base of the tail

Full the ears

58

Calf

MATERIALS

legs: 3/100 in (0.8 mm) copper wire, 2 pieces
    each 5 in (13 cm) long
head/neck: 3/4 x 4 1/4 in (2 x 11 cm)
ears: 3/8 x 1 1/4 in (1 x 3 cm) (2 pieces)
tail: 3/8 x 4 in (1 x 10 cm)
1/2 oz (13 g) white, brown, skin- and beige-
    coloured merino/sheep's wool
white curly wool

Make the body relatively short, the legs longer.
The neck should be thinner than for the Cow,
the head short and the forehead round. Make the
back slope downwards from the tail to the neck.
Bend the neck upwards slightly and shape the
forehead nicely rounded. While still wet, needle
felt nostrils and mouth (see page 77).

Shape the chest and neck curved

Full a round head

Horse

MATERIALS

legs: 1/16 in (1.5 mm) copper wire, 2 pieces
    each 8 in (20 cm) long
head/neck: 1 1/2 x 6 1/4 in (4 x 16 cm)
ears: 1/2 x 1 1/2 in (1.5 x 4 cm) (2 pieces)
1 1/2 oz (45 g) beige, brown mountain sheep's wool
beige, grey merino wool
brown curly wool

Twist the wire to make the back legs at least 1/2 in (1.5 cm) longer than the front legs. Make the chest fat and the backside round. Keep the legs sturdy. Add lots of thin strands around the stomach and sides. Make the ears small and pointy, but not too thin. While fulling, press the back downwards in the centre, make the thighs clearly visible and pull out the back legs (they usually slip too far into the body). Full the sides of the head narrower at eye level. Needle felt nostrils and a mouth line while still wet (see page 77). Once dry, needle felt mane, tail and leg hair in place (see page 79).

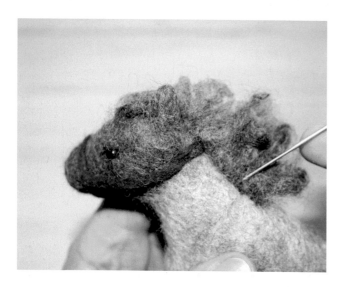

Needle felt the mane in place

Needle felt hoof tufts in place

Donkey

MATERIALS

legs: 3/100 in (0.8 mm) copper wire, 2 pieces
   each 6 in (15 cm) long
head/neck: 1 x 5 1/2 in (2.5 x 14 cm)
tail: 3/8 x 4 3/4 in (1 x 12 cm)
ears: 3/4 x 3 1/8 in (2 x 8 cm) (2 pieces)
1/2 oz (13 g) grey brown, dark brown, white,
   brown merino/sheep's wool
grey curly wool

Make the body relatively short, the legs thin, the backside round but not too fat, the stomach round and the chest quite thin. Make large ears with an obvious fold and the head quite large with a round forehead and cheek bones. Wind a tuft around the thin tail. Use brown wool for the hooves, tufts of hair and along the back; cover mouth and stomach with white wool. Full a slightly hollow back, bend the neck backwards, and shape the stomach round. At eye level, full the head thinner from the top and sides, this makes a rounded forehead and lower jaw. Full the neck thinner at the sides under the head. Needle felt nostrils and mouth line while wet (see page 77).

Optionally, you can cut open the mouth with a sharp pair of scissors, then re-felt. Fold the ears lengthwise and rub between your fingers, taper towards the tips.

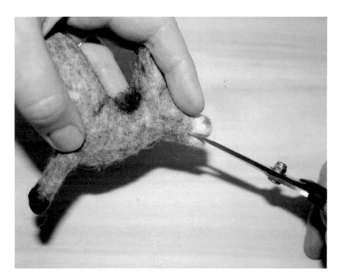

Cut the mouth open

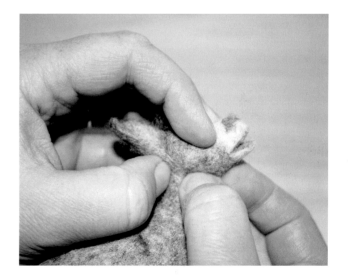

Shape the head round from top and bottom

61

Billy goat or goat

Materials

legs: $3/100$ in (0.8 mm) copper wire
billy goat: 2 pieces each 4 $3/4$ in (12 cm) long
goat: 2 pieces each 4 in (10.5 cm) long
chest/neck: $1/2$ x 4 $1/4$ in (1.5 x 11 cm)
ears: $3/8$ x 1 $1/4$ in (1 x 3 cm) (2 pieces)
horns (billy goat): $3/8$ x 4 in (1 x 10 cm)
horns (goat): $1/16$ x 2 in (0.5 x 5 cm)
tail: $3/8$ x 2 in (1 x 5 cm)
$1/3$ oz (10 g) black, grey merino/sheep's wool for
  the billy goat
$1/4$ oz (7 g) brown, white, dark brown merino/
  sheep's wool for the goat
brown or black curly wool for the beard

Make the body square, the stomach round. Add the ears to the still quite small head, and needle felt the horns in place. Attach the ears and horns to the head at the same time. Make short thin horns for the goat, long thick horns for the billy goat. The head should be relatively short and thin. Add a short, thin tail. Press the whole muzzle downwards while fulling so that the head is sloping downwards. Shape the thighs so they are clearly visible.

Needle felt horns in place

Sheep

MATERIALS

legs: $3/100$ in (0.8 mm) copper wire, 2 pieces each 4 $1/2$ in (11.5 cm) long
chest/neck: $1/2$ x 4 $1/4$ in (1.5 x 11 cm)
ears: $3/8$ x 1 $1/4$ in (1 x 3 cm) (2 pieces)
tail: $3/8$ x 2 $3/4$ in (1 x 7 cm)
$1/4$ oz (6 g) white merino/sheep's wool
$1/6$ oz (4 g) white curly wool

Add lots of layers of wool to the body. Make the head quite long and thin, the legs thin. Don't forget the chest and backside. Attach the long thin tail, add a few pieces of wool to it. Place curly wool densely over one side of the body, felt in place and then add more wool to the other side in the same way. Once dry you can pull out the curls with a sewing needle — or you can needle felt a further thin layer of curly wool on top.

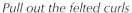
Pull out the felted curls

Miniature animals

Note: making these animals requires very fine motor skills.

Blackbird, rabbit, swallow, kitten, mouse, chicks and ducklings, teddy bear

Use less than $1/32$ oz (1 g) fine merino wool and do not make the thin starting pieces larger than $3/8 \times 1 \, 1/4$ in (1 x 3 cm). Pull out the beak, tail or ears, or needle felt very thin pieces of wool in place; wet it all. Use a few short and thin pieces of wool to construct the body. Add the appropriate colours or spots and felt between the tips of your fingers.

Full the teddy bear sitting down and its muzzle from above. Carefully cuddle towards the centre so that it is not too thin and stiff.

Ear wool pieces (above), add the mouth

One ear added, the other ear wool piece

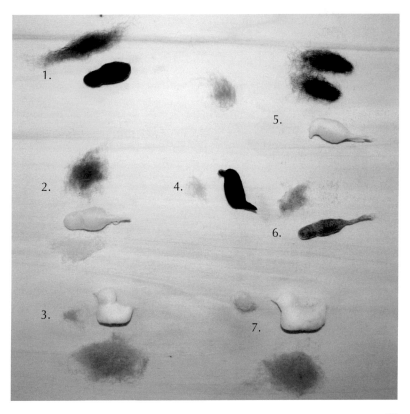

1. Rabbit body with ear wool piece
2. Kitten body with ear and wool for the spot
3. Chick body with beak and feather wool
4. Blackbird body with beak wool
5. Swallow body with beak and wing wool
6. Mouse body with ear wool
7. Duckling body with bill and feather wool

Human figures

Mum

MATERIALS

body wire: 3/100 in (0.8 mm) copper wire, 7 in
    (18 cm) long
head/arms wire: 3/100 in (0.8 mm) copper wire,
    6 1/4 in (16 cm) long
head: 3/4 x 5 in (2 x 13 cm)
arms/hands: 3/16 x 3 1/8 in (0.5 x 8 cm)
3/8 oz (11 g) skin-coloured, white, light grey,
    mottled orange, brown merino wool
reddish-brown curly wool for the hair

Twist a loop 3/8 in (1 cm) circumference into the
centre of the short (head/arms) wire, for the head.
Wind the longer piece of wire (body wire) around
the neck from the back and twist twice below the
arms.

66

Push a strand of wool 3/4 in (2 cm) through the **head** loop and wind tightly around it, add one or two short strands until the head is at least 3/4 in (2 cm) circumference. Wind a skin-coloured strand around the head.

For the **hands and arms**, wind a very thin strand four times around the ends of the hand wire for approximately 3/16 in (0.5 cm), bend the wire back and wind the rest of the wool around the hands and arms. Make the **feet** in the same way.

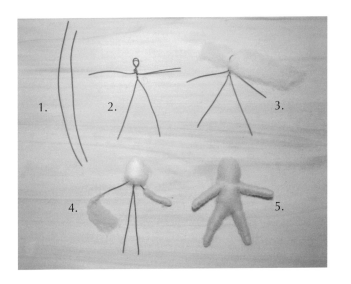

1. Wire pieces
2. Finished body frame
3. Head wool pushed through the head loop
4. Wound head, winding around the arms
5. Almost finished body

Bend back the wire ends

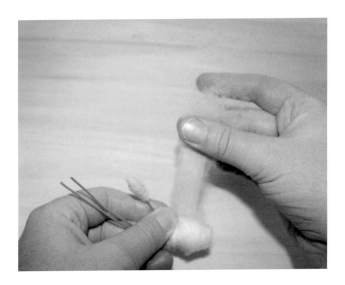

Wind skin-coloured wool over the head

Wind evenly, firmly and thinly around the whole frame. Do not wind too tightly or too loosely. Make the thighs and upper arms slightly fatter.

Build up the **torso** using white wool, then wind skin-coloured wool over it all and connect to arms and legs. Connect the head to the body at the front and back with a wide piece of wool. Place several additional pieces of wool over the nose/mouth to be made into a good chin/cheek area later. Place a skin-coloured piece of wool on

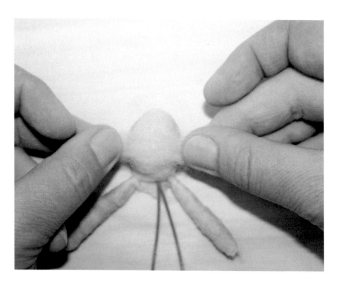

Add chin wool

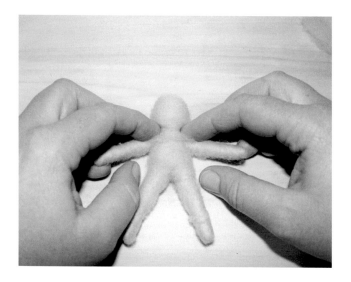

Connect the head and body

Body finished, pant (trouser) wool beside it

Put the pants (trousers) on

top of the head. Add a suitable hair colour for the provisional hair style.

Check whether arms and legs are even and have been wound fat enough. Due to the wire framework, the figure only shrinks thinner while fulling, not shorter. Felt everything well.

For the **clothes**, wind the grey piece of wool around the lower body, make the pant (trouser) legs and wind them around the legs. Fold down the waistband and the pant (trouser) legs up and

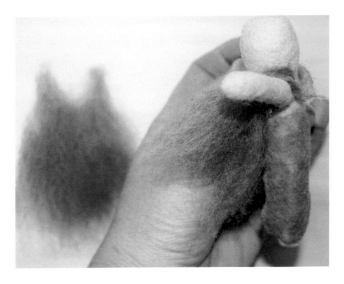

Add the front of the top

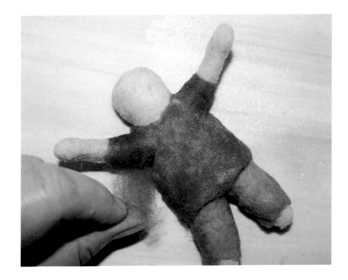

Wind short sleeves, connecting arms and body

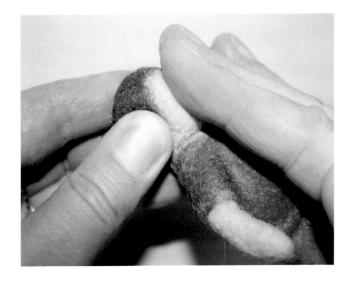

Full the face

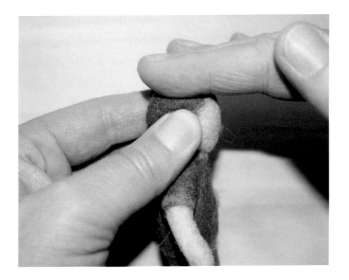

Full the top of the head

felt in place. Tease the orange wool into two same-sized pieces. Tease one end into two thin strands and place these over the shoulders beside the neck (not over the arms!). Fold back the lower edge and smooth the sides to the back. Make the back in the same way. Wind short sleeves, connect shoulders and armpits to the sleeves. Add extra colour for decoration as you wish and felt everything well. Rub the arms and legs from the side. Wind brown shoe wool around the feet — add some short pieces

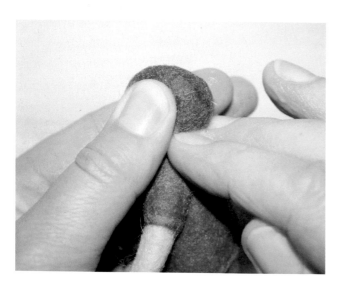

Full the nape of the neck

Full the neck

Full the eye line

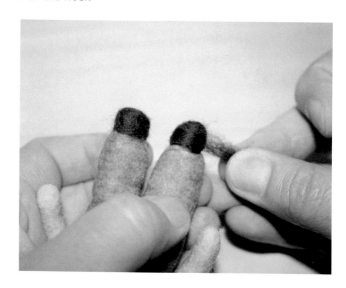

Wind the shoes on

70

to the front of the shoe, felt and full. If the feet are already well felted and you move the shoes back and forth while felting, they do not felt to the feet and can be taken off later. Hold the head at the side and full the front and top. If necessary, push some of the wool downwards to make a good chin. Make the back of the head; full the eye line with your finger tips or a ruler. If you want, you can pull out a nose with a large needle while the wool is still wet. Then felt again, circling from above. Needle felt the hair in place once the doll is dry (see page 80).

Pin the nose

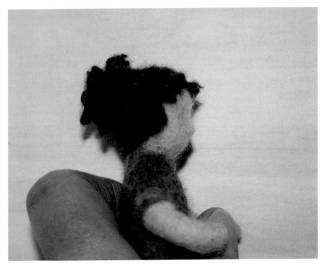

Nose pulled out

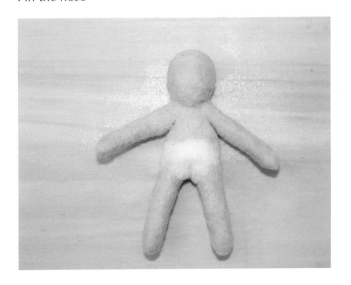

Underpants for a girl

Dress piece, placed on a girl

Measurements for other human figures

Use ³/₁₀₀ in (0.8 mm) copper wire
The first measurement is the length of the body/
    legs wire
The second measurement is the length of the
    head/arms wire
1/4 to ³/8 oz (7 to 11 g) merino wool

DAD

7 3/4 / 5 1/2 in (20 / 14 cm), white, skin-
    coloured, dark blue, pastel green, brown
brown pieces for hair and beard

OLDER DAUGHTER, MARY

5 1/2 / 4 in (14 / 10 cm), white, skin-coloured,
    mottled multicoloured, dark red, yellow
sand-coloured wool batt for hair

SON, SIMON
5 / 3 ½ in (13 / 9 cm), white, skin-coloured,
    dark blue, light blue, brown
light brown wool for hair

YOUNGER DAUGHTER, LUCY
4 / 2 ³/₈ in (10 / 6 cm), white, skin coloured,
    rose pink, bright pink
light yellow curly wool for hair

NEIGHBOURING GIRL, ANNIE
4 ¾ / 3 ¹/₈ in (12 / 8 cm), white, skin-coloured,
    mottled multicoloured, yellow, brown
yellow curls for hair

NEIGHBOURING BOY, TOM
5 / 3 ½ in (13 / 9 cm), white, skin-coloured,
    dark blue, grey, brown
yellow-beige wool batt for hair

Little gnome (tomten)

MATERIALS

body wire: $^1/100$ in (0.5 mm) copper wire, 3 $^1/2$
   in (9 cm) long
head/arms wire: $^1/100$ in (0.5 mm) copper wire,
   2 in (5 cm) long
$^1/6$ oz (4 g) beige, grey, green, mottled rust,
   brown merino wool
white pieces for the beard

Wind a tight small roll for the nose, $^3/16$ x $^3/8$ in
(0.5 x 1 cm), and place in the centre of the head.
Add a piece of wool over the nose and the head.
Add some more wool beneath the nose and build
up forehead and cheeks. Wind the shoes, then
wind grey leg wool over the brown top of the
shoe.

Fold back the bottom side of the triangular
pointed hat piece and wind tightly around the
head. Place it directly above the nose and deep
into the neck. Add more wool to the tip. Needle
felt in place while dry, then carefully wet felt it.
Full the nose thinner towards the base, this leaves
space for the eyes. Needle felt the beard in place
once dry (see page 80).

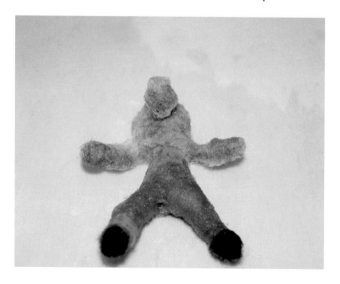

Nose roll added

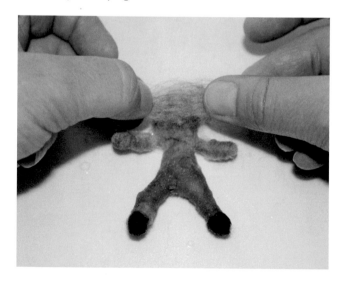

Attach the nose with wool piece

74

Finished body with hat wool piece

Wind the hat around the head

Wind around the hat tip

Full the large nose

Clothes and accessories

Make the clothes about one third larger than the desired finished size. Felt the jacket, hat and galoshes (wellington boots) around a bubble wrap template. To make them, place a thin piece of wool batt, slightly larger than the template, over the template, wet, turn around and stroke the overhanging bits of wool around the template. Repeat this process for the other side. Felt as described, full well and then cut open and shape. Make the apron and the washing for the washing line flat over a template and stroke the edges inwards. Alternatively cut them out of a piece of thin felt.

Teased out clothes with template

Finishing Touches

Before the projects are dry

Needle felting mouth and nostrils

MATERIALS

fine felting needle
sponge

Animals with a soft nose and mouth (for example, Cow, Horse, Donkey, Pig) look good if the nostrils and mouth line are needle felted. The outlines are clearer if needle felted while still wet. First pre-shape the nostrils with your finger, and then make them into a crescent shape. Needle felt the mouth line with the needle held very flat. Pinch the mouth together to make a clearer line.

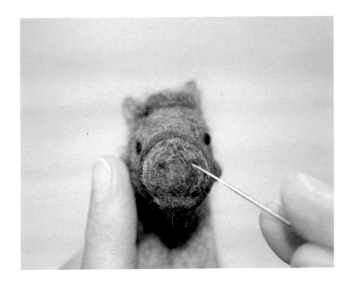

Needle felt nostrils

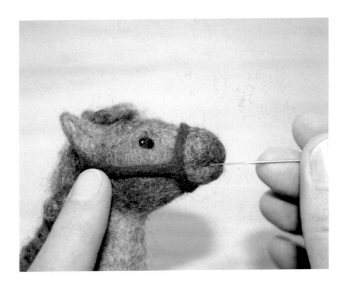

Needle felt mouth line

Needle felting eyes and nose

MATERIALS
black, white, green, blue, brown fine merino
   wool
fine felting needle
sponge

If you don't want to embroider the eyes, it's best
to needle felt them in place while the animal is
still wet and then re-felt over them, as this makes
them smoother and connects them to the head
well. Place a tiny piece of wool (do not roll up)
on the eye. Needle felt in place through the
centre with a fine felting needle. Poke the fibres
at the edges into the centre. Only then needle
felt the edges and make a hollow around the eye.
Optionally, add a small dot of light, which gives
a more three-dimensional effect to the eye. Place
a sponge under the object when needle felting to
avoid injury and the needle breaking.

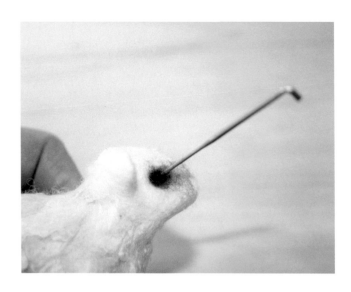

Place and attach eye wool

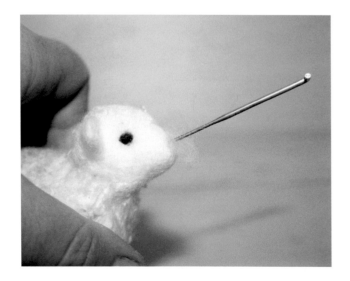

Add nose wool

Needle felt nose wool in place

78

Rinsing out the soap

After felting you need to rinse the soap out thoroughly. To do this, shower the finished felted object for 10 seconds every 10 minutes (the showering intervals can also be longer). Do not press, squeeze or reshape during this process. Optionally, you can place the object in vinegar water for 5 minutes (a bowl with water and a squirt of vinegar essence or white vinegar). Let the water drip out and place on a towel. Once the felted object is damp (but only then) it can — if necessary — be knocked into shape, and bent and pushed into the desired position. Leave to dry in a warm place.

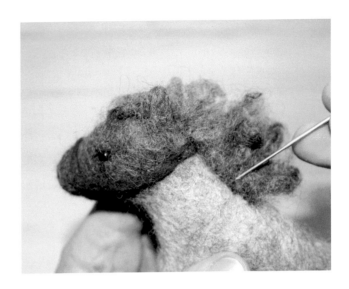

Needle felt the mane

After the projects are dry

Needle felting hair

MATERIALS

yellow, beige, light brown, red brown, dark brown, black, white short and longer curly wool, or fine wool batt, or roving (depending on project)

MANE AND TAIL

To needle felt in place, always needle felt the curls deep into the head, neck or backside in the direction of the fibres. For the tail, repeatedly poke in different directions to give a firmer hold. To make a tail tuft, place short pieces around the tail and needle felt in place. If the curls are too long, cut them shorter, tease out the ends and only then needle felt them in place.

Needle felt the tail

Short hair can be needle felted in place along a left or right parting or from the centre of the back outwards in a star shape, using thin strands or curls. Leave small gaps here and there and fill them with a short piece of wool. Leave a few strands standing up at the forehead or back of the head.

To make **braids**, place a wide strand or several curls over the back and top of the head. Needle felt a parting along the top and back of the head. Tie or plait two braids above the ears. Needle felt the braid base to the head.

Needle felt **long hair** starting at the back whorl. Place very long curls over the top of the head and needle felt along the parting or add shorter curls from the left and right and needle felt the ends into the head along the parting.

To make a **hair knot**, needle felt a star shape as for short hair, leave gaps and fill with short curls. Leave single curls hanging out. Wind the curls around the back whorl and style by needle felting in place.

Place a **beard** in a slight curve up to the ears and poke with the needle, slanting from below.

If the curls are too long, you can cut them, tease the ends and then needle felt them in place.

If you have small children in your house, you can also sew the hair to the head for a more secure hold.

Needle felt a hair knot

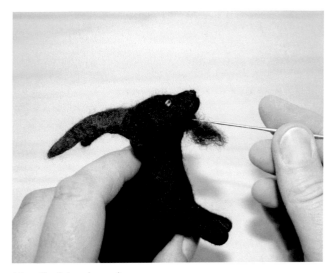

Needle felt a beard

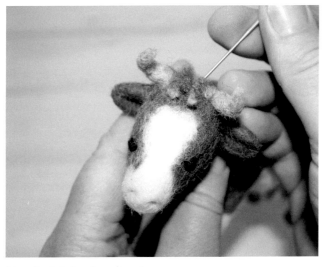

Needle felt forehead curls

Embroidering eyes and mouth

MATERIALS

dark brown, black, green, blue, pink, white
    cotton darning or embroidery thread
thin sewing needle
scissors
three black pins
fine black, water resistant felt-tip pen

Mark the place for the eyes and the mouth with pins. Sew a small stitch using two threads for the muzzle. After several crosswise stitches beside and over each other, sew a longer or shorter lengthwise stitch, depending on the type of animal.

Again depending on animal, sew two longer or shorter slanting stitches for the mouth. Then push the needle up to the left eye. First hint at the eyes left and right with short stitches, then sew several stitches beside and over each other until they're the right size. To finish, bring the needle out away from the head and sew the end in place by inserting the needle back into the same hole and bringing it out again just beside it.

A white light dot looks good on dark eyes. Sew two tiny stitches at the side of the eye using white thread. Draw or sew a black pupil into light coloured eyes with a fine water resistant felt-tip pen or thread.

Mark the eyes and nose with pins

82

The Farmyard

Wool and other materials

4 1/2 lb (2 kg) beige and medium brown
  mountain sheep's wool
1 lb (500 g) different shades of green, 1 lb (500 g)
  different shades of red merino/sheep's wool
2/3 oz (20 g) brown, 1 2/3 oz (50 g) grey, 2/3 oz
  (25 g) blue merino/sheep's wool
7 oz (200 g) grey and brown mountain sheep's
  wool
7 oz (200 g) different coloured curly wool
1/3 oz (10 g) different coloured wool-silk roving

large working table (countertop), approximately
  6 1/2 x 4 ft (2 x 1.3 m)
large piece of bubble wrap, approximately 8 x 6 ft
  (2.5 x 1.8 m) (for the whole farmyard)
a selection of smaller and larger cardboard
  boxes
cling film (plastic wrap), plastic sheet or rubbish
  (garbage) bag
adhesive tape, measuring tape
large bowl, whisk, soft soap, hot water
water sprayer or small watering can
sponge, towels, large towel

felting board
single and triple felting needle holder
fine and medium felting needles, pins, large
  darning needle, crocheting needle
leather hole punch
sharp scissors, knife, optional scalpel
large marble, table tennis ball, small glass

The process of building a farmyard is similar to building a real house: first you have to plan, then organise the materials, and then make sufficient space and time.

Making the entire farmyard is a large project that will take 3 to 5 full days. It's best if there are two people working on it together, so plan for a creative holiday!

However, you can felt the farmyard in different sections, for example, a stable with a shelter and a field; followed later by a farmhouse with a baking house, dog kennel and garden; followed later still by a hen house with a water fountain, fence, tree and lake. This way you can also add to the farmyard later when you have another spare day.

Day 1: preliminary building work

MATERIALS

starting piece: 1 1/2 lb (700 g) mountain sheep's wool, about 6 x 3 1/2 ft (1.8 x 1.1 m)

Cardboard box measurements (approximate, length x breadth x height)
stable: 12 1/4 x 9 1/2 x 9 in (31 x 24 x 23 cm)
lean-to shelter: 8 1/4 x 6 x 7 1/4 in (21 x 15 x 18 cm)
farmhouse: 15 x 10 x 9 in (38 x 25 x 23 cm)
baking house: 4 x 4 x 3 in (10 x 10 x 8 cm)
dog kennel: 2 3/8 x 1 1/4 x 2 in (6 x 3 x 5 cm)
hen house: 7 x 5 x 6 in (18 x 13 x 15 cm)
water fountain: 3 1/8 x 1 1/2 x 1 1/4 in (8 x 4 x 3 cm)

Roll up the sides of a plastic sheet (or rubbish/garbage bag) until it measures 6 1/2 x 4 ft (2 x 1.3 m). Hold the edges in place with adhesive tape or pegs. Wrap cling film (plastic wrap) around the cardboard boxes and stick in place with adhesive tape. Irregularly tear the basic measurements, approximately 6 x 3 1/2 ft (1.8 x 1.1 m), out of the wool batt and place the wool onto the plastic sheet. This is the basic 'groundwork.' Arrange the cardboard boxes over the base as you please. Tease out long strands of wool from the wool batt, at least as long as the cardboard box's circumferences and slightly wider than their height. Wind the strands tightly around the cardboard boxes and needle felt the sides together with a triple felting needle. Needle felt around the base of the house well. Repeat this process with a second layer of wool batt. Tease out the lower edge and attach well to the base. Fold back the top of the long side of house wall.

Slowly pull up the gable wall of the stable, farmhouse, baking house and the dog kennel until the gable ends can nearly touch one another in the middle of the cardboard box when folded down.

Now it's good for two people to work together. Prepare 4 litres of soapy water and fill a small watering can or water sprayer. Add two to three layers of wool to each house wall and smooth down. One person can water while the other felts

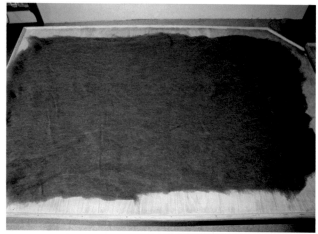

Wool batt forms the groundwork

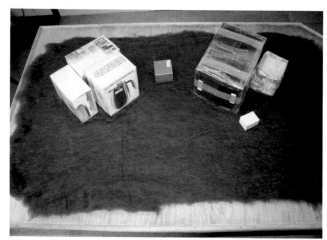

Add cardboard boxes for the buildings

in place. Fold the upper edges downwards and let the lower edges merge into the base. Place two layers over the ground in the stable, baking house, dog kennel and hen house, and connect to the inner wall.

Needle felt a 8 1/4 x 6 1/4 in (21 x 15 cm) large piece of wool batt to one long side of the stable, add another brown and rust–brown layer, wet and connect. Felt well, particularly the connecting edges.

Place two to three layers of wool over the hen house (see also the instructions for Rabbit Hutch, page 20) and cut the roof out like a flap. Place rust–coloured wool thickly over it, needle felt in place and wet felt well. Add two layers of brown wool to the water fountain and felt.

Soak up superfluous water with a large sponge whenever necessary.

Pull out the gable ends

Needle felt two layers over the walls

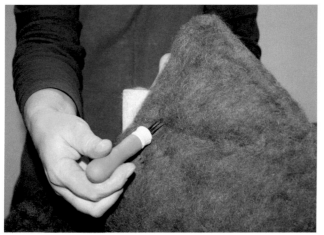

Connect the edges with a triple felting needle and sponge

Check the gable measurements

Day 2: adding landscape and detail

Push the unfelted lower edge of the cut-in-half fence posts (page 93) through the wool batt base, spread their base apart, close the fleece around the hole again and cover well with a layer of wool. Repeat this process with the four posts for the lean-to shelter (next to the stable). Place brown curly wool over the ground of the shelter.

Add at least three posts in the stable in the same way. Place a post behind the water fountain for the tap. Add thin posts between the living quarters and the hen house.

Build a small wall for the toilet inside the house. First needle felt it in place, then wet it and felt. Place two layers of beige wool over the floor of the house and felt it all in place well.

If you want bushes and trees firmly attached

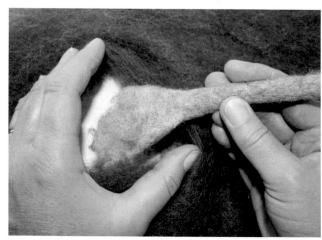

Add a fence post

to the ground, 'plant' them in place in the same way as for the posts. Use grey curly wool for paths and the courtyard. Add green wool to the field and make meadow flowers with yellow and green curly wool. Make the garden in front of the water fountain. Knot strips of wool roving into the ground to make long grasses and stems. To do this, push a crocheting hook through the wool base, bring it back up 3/8 in (1 cm) away, hook up the roving and pull through. Green curly wool, needle felted thickly to the base, makes good lettuce heads. Needle felt flowers onto the fields using curly wool. For a herb garden, needle felt thick layers of different coloured curly wool to the ground.

Make the lake using teased apart, blue curly wool, and knot reeds in place. Add a few wound ovals as stones or bushes (page 94) and connect to

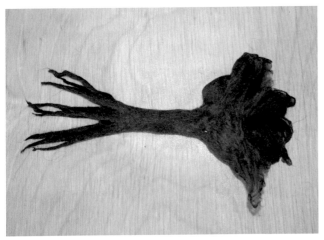

A small tree

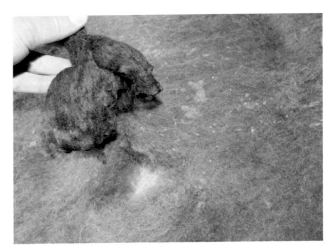

Push the tree into the prepared batt

Felt the house walls well, plant trees and bushes, place stones and bushes on the ground, put the path in place

Build the water fountain

the ground with two thin layers of wool batt. Put grey or green wool over them and any decoration you wish. Add the wound dung heap in the same way, then add a thick layer of brown curly wool.

Place green or coloured wool over all the remaining areas of bare ground. Felt the posts, bushes, trees and grasses well. Wet bit by bit with hot soapy water and felt on with your flat hand or a thin plastic sheet. Once the wool is well connected, rub, shove and roll from the outside to the inside, first folding down the fence posts and small bushes. Fold the wet house walls inwards and roll and push together carefully as much as possible. Also work from the other side, rubbing and working with the felting board. On the whole, everything should shrink by at least

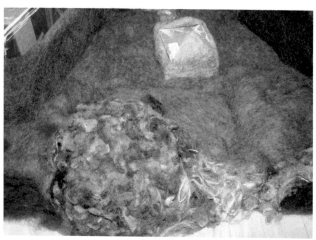

Build up the dung heap

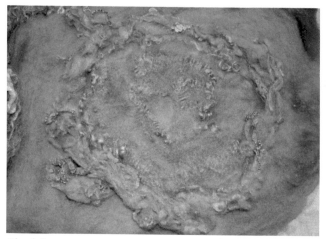

The lake

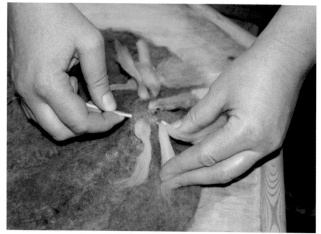

Knot reeds into place

Place colour over all remaining bare ground, apart from the garden

30%. You can take a break while fulling at any point. To finish, pour hot water over everything and either soak it up with a sponge or let it drip away. Place towels around the edges.

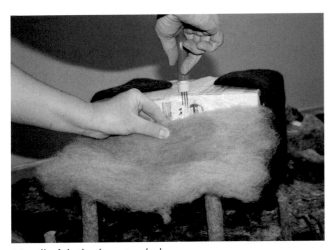

Needle felt the lean-to shelter

Arrange the garden

Felt everything well (houses not yet fulled)

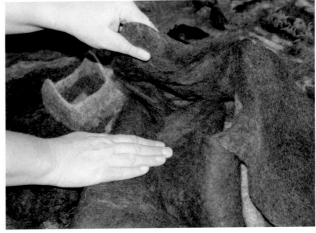

Fold the house flat for fulling

Day 3: finishing and fine details

Pour hot soapy water over it all again to finish fulling. Felt the edges well using a felting board. Mark the windows and doors with pins or a felt-tip pen. Cut the doors with a scalpel and cut out the windows. Use sharp scissors for the corners. Cut slanting edges into too thick walls. Re-felt all the cut edges, including the door step, to make them flat and solid.

Place the entire piece in the bathtub, including the sheet, and shower several times well (you could also do this outdoors). Add a squirt of vinegar into the last rinsing water. Let the water drip away and place on a towel. You can now push anything still squint into shape, smooth wavy bits and straighten trees and grasses. Leave to dry in a warm place.

Cut out the door

Cut out the window

Individual details

Roofs

Felting the roofs can be done separately from the main work. Older children can help to roll the felt.

MATERIALS
farmhouse roof
21 1/2 x 21 1/2 in (54 x 54 cm)
17 x 17 in (43 x 43 cm), 2 layers brown, 1 1/2
   layers mottled red mountain sheep's wool
chimney, see page 92

stable roof
21 3/4 x 21 1/4 in (55 x 51 cm)
17 1/2 x 16 in (44 x 40 cm) 2 layers of brown,
   1 1/2 layers mottled red mountain sheep's wool

baking house roof
11 x 10 1/2 in (28 x 27 cm)
7 x 6 3/4 in (18 x 17 cm) 1 layer mottled red
   sheep's wool
chimney, see page 92

dog kennel roof
6 3/4 x 6 in (17 x 15 cm)
4 3/4 x 4 in (12 x 10 cm) 1/2 layer red merino
   wool

Put the roof starting piece on the bubble wrap, wet well and felt using a plastic sheet if necessary. Add the chimney (see page 92) to the farmhouse and baking house roofs before wetting them.

Roll up with the bubble wrap and carefully roll; repeat this process from all directions. Once the felt is firmer, roll it in a wet towel and roll with pressure. Repeat in all eight directions (also turning the piece over) until you have the desired shape. If necessary, cut the edges straight. Cut a section out of the side of the roofs for the stable and hen house, where the lean-to structures will go. Re-felt all the edges well. Slightly irregular edges can be straightened in the following way: rub bulges inwards and pull indentations outwards. Finally, fold the roof in half and felt the roof ridge.

Chimney

MATERIALS

starting piece (pipe): 2 3/4 x 2 3/4 in (7 x 7 cm)
cowl: 2 3/4 x 1 1/2 in (7 x 4 cm)
1/16 oz (1.5 g) (baking house), 1/12 oz (2.5 g)
  (farmhouse) black merino wool

The farmhouse and baking house have a chimney. Wind the starting piece to make the chimney pipe, wet and tease one end apart. Wind the cowl wool around two fingers, pinch the top shut, wet and place on top of the chimney pipe (like a mushroom hat on a stem). Connect with a few layers of wool from below. Felt well, apart from the base, before attaching it to the roof. Push it through a hole in the unfelted roof (see also instructions for Fence posts), close the roof wool around the hole and cover well with a layer of red wool. Felt this area well first. While fulling the roof, bend the chimney down flat.

Chimney pipe with cowl pieces

Push the chimney into the roof hole

Planted trees

MATERIALS

starting piece: 15 3/4 x 15 3/4 in (40 x 40 cm)
5 1/4 oz (150 g) brown mountain sheep's wool,
    green curly wool

Roll up the starting piece tightly, wet the centre
and felt. Divide one end into 5 to 7 roots, then
divide them again into smaller roots. Make the
trunk broader towards the roots (see image bottom
left on page 16). Wind a plastic bag around the
roots and knot its ends to stop the roots felting;
this means you can still felt them to the ground
later. Divide the top end into 5 large branches.
Separate them again into smaller twigs and wind
a few layers of wool diagonally around them. Felt
the trunk and treetop well, full and shape. Cut a
knothole and re-felt the cut edges. Once the tree
is felted and dried, needle felt green curly wool
for leaves.

Posts for the lean-to shelter, fence posts and fence rails

MATERIALS

starting piece (fence post): 4 3/4 x 8 in (12 x 20 cm)
starting piece (fence rails): 1 1/4 x 24 in (3 x 60 cm)
starting piece (shelter post): 8 x 14 in (20 x 35 cm)
5 1/4 oz (150 g) beige mountain sheep's wool
1 oz (30 g) beige mountain sheep's wool roving
    or fleece

Roll up tightly lengthwise and gently felt. Leave
the ends dry so you can felt them into the base
later. Full the centre part well using not much
water. Cut in half. If necessary, you can change
the length later by cutting the tops off. Felt one
long fence rail and pull it through holes in the
fence posts.

1. Post   2. Fulled post, cut in half

Make holes in the posts and thread thin fence rails through

Stones and dung heap

MATERIALS

starting pieces: 8 x 5 in (20 x 13 cm), 16 x 10 in
   (40 x 25 cm)
1 oz (30 g) grey merino/sheep's wool
1 2/3 oz (50 g) brown mountain sheep's wool
   and curly wool

For a **stone**, roll up the starting piece widthwise tightly and fold the edges inwards. Wet, place where you want, attach to the base and add grey wool. Or, to felt a separate stone, wind a strand around it lengthwise, cover with stone coloured wool and felt.

To make a **bush**, use a larger starting piece of wool and cover with green curly wool, felt to the ground or felt separately.

For a **dung heap**, add additional wool layers to the lower half of the rolled up dung heap wool to make it cone shaped. Place the heap onto the wool base, attach to the base with two large layers of wool and cover with brown curly wool. Felt well.

Wind the stones

Finishing touches once the farmyard is dry

This is the time to let your creativity loose! Children and grandparents can also help. Using a fine felting needle in a needle holder, needle felt ramblers, ivy, grape vines, flowers, leaves, roses or hollyhocks wherever you please. Curly wool or wool/silk roving is most suitable.

You can also needle felt the swallow's nest in place (see image on p.114). Use coloured dots for the swallow chicks. Sew or needle felt the swallow to the nest.

Sew a seam along the roof ridge with six-ply cotton embroidery thread. Sew simple large running stitches from one gable side to the other, then sew back again along the seam exactly filling the spaces.

Climbing roses needle felted in place

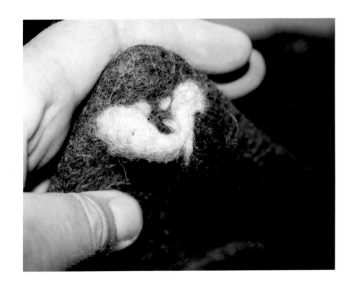

Swallow's nest

Sew roof ridge

95

Household items

Note: making these animals requires very fine motor skills.

<small/>

MATERIALS
white, light blue, dark grey, grey, anthracite-
    colour, brown, yellow merino wool
black mountain sheep's wool for the stove
large glass ball
table tennis (ping pong) ball
cylindrical glass
solid template

MUG
Tease white and light blue wool together and place thinly over both sides of a solid template, 1 $^1/_2$ x $^1/_2$ in (4 x 1.5 cm). Felt well, cut in half and full both mugs around a thin pencil to finish.

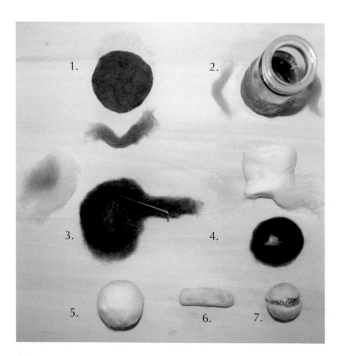

1. Lid with handle
2. Pot with two handles
3. Frying pan with fried egg wool
4. Toilet with toilet seat
5. Bowl
6. Plate
7. Mug

PLATE

Place three thin layers of white and light blue wool around a large marble. Felt, then cut in half around the centre. Full around the marble. To finish, shape the base flat.

BOWL

Place three thin white layers around a table tennis (ping pong) ball and felt well. Cut a small circle out of the top. Take the ball out, fill the bowl with foam or wool and needle felt light blue dots to it. Reinsert the ball and felt again; stroke the edge downwards. Flatten the base slightly.

FRYING PAN WITH EGGS

Take a piece of anthracite-coloured wool and pull a pan handle out of one side. Bend the edges inwards and anchor with the felting needle. Add one or two pieces of wool to the base of the handle. Keep bending the edges upwards while felting. Needle felt first the white of the fried eggs, then the yellow and full together to finish.

POT

Wind light grey strands of wool around a cylindrical glass or tin, 1 1/2 in (4 cm) circumference. Place a piece of wool over the base and felt everything. Remove the glass to needle felt the handle in place. Carefully finish felting. Make a circle for the lid, felt slightly, needle felt the lid handle in place and finish felting, shaping it slightly curved.

STOVE

Wind cling film (plastic wrap) around a cardboard box 3 1/8 x 1 1/2 x 2 3/8 in (8 x 4 x 6 cm). Wind black mountain sheep's wool in long strands twice around the narrower sides. Fold down the edge. Place two oval pieces of wool batt over the top, then fold back the edges, leaving 1/2 in (1.5 cm) overhanging. Anchor the stove top to the body. Felt everything well, remove the box and continue fulling. Needle felt the hotplates and the oven door using grey wool and felt again. Cut a hole into the centre back of the stove for the stove pipe. Roll up a 6 x 4 in (15 x 10 cm) piece of dark grey merino wool lengthwise, felt, full and push into the stove as a stove pipe.

Stove pipe, not felted, stove top folded back

TOILET

Wind white strands of wool around two fingers, then fold back the upper edge. Wind around the lower half (without using your fingers) to make it narrower. Place a small piece of wool into the bowl at the bottom and add another wool piece to the sides. Cover any creases and carefully felt and shape.

Wind a brown strand of wool into an O shape, then wind small pieces of wool around it from above and wet. Felt the O shape and sew or glue (hot glue gun) to the toilet seat once dry.

FINISHING ACCESSORIES

You can often buy other items such as a milking pail, bucket, watering can, spade, shovel, hammer, axe and small baskets at stores which sell doll's house accessories. Many toy stores sell toy tractors.

A Day on the Farm

It is a crisp, clear morning in spring.

The birds are singing.

Everything else is still quiet.

Dad is already milking the cows in the barn.

Mum also gets up early. She is making dough for bread, because today is baking day.

The cat meows by the front door. Soon it can come in and have breakfast.

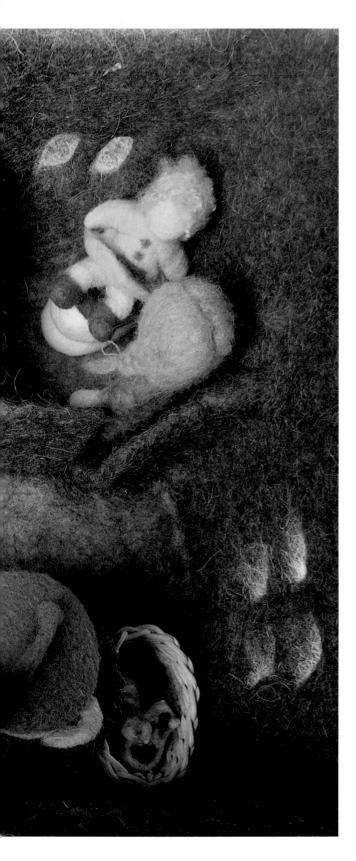

The children are just getting up.

Lucy can already go to the toilet all by herself. But Mary still looks after her.

Simon calls out to the baby kitten. He is actually supposed to set the table for breakfast.

Dad reads the paper and discusses all the things to do today with Mum.

The cows are mooing impatiently in the stable. They want to be let out into the fields.

But first Dad and Simon feed the pigs. The water troughs are filled with fresh water.

The goose goes off to the lake with her goslings.

The cows gently walk out of the stable.

The horse Max neighs 'hello'. He spent the night alone in the meadow and is looking forward to some company.

After the dog Sandy has been fed, Mum gets a bucket and heads off to check on the sheep and goats with the girls.

The lambs gambol and jump around joyfully. The mother animals get extra oats, and the water troughs are filled with fresh water.

The little kid jumps up close to Lucy. Mary feeds the goat with a branch.

The donkey brays 'ee-aw' loudly five times. He wants to go out into the field. But first Dad has to fix the fence, otherwise the donkey will escape and eat the flowers and vegetables in the garden.

Mary throws him an armful of hay over the fence.

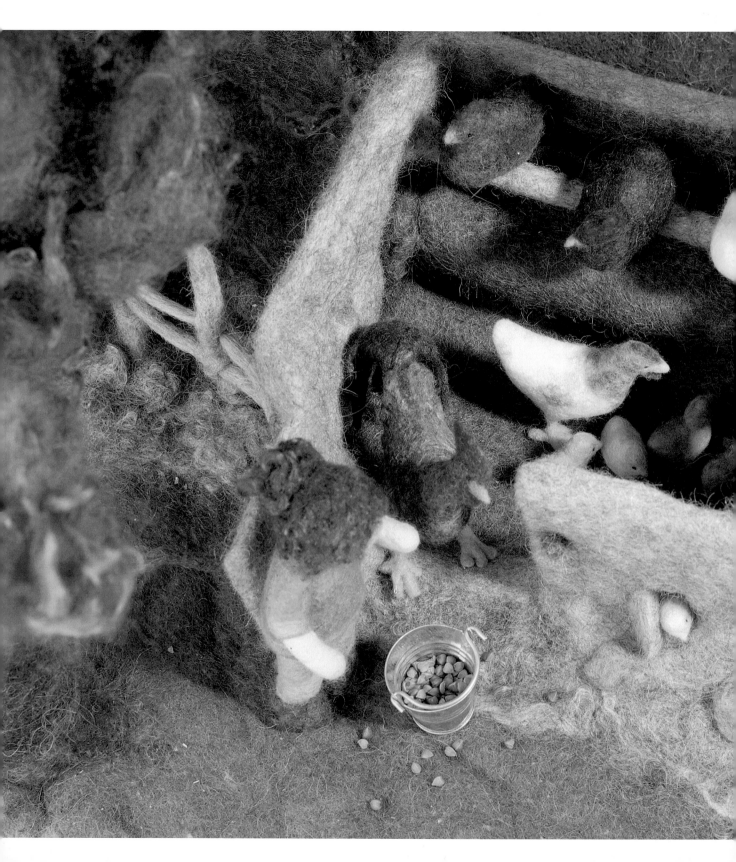

Mum opens the hen house.

First the rooster comes out, then the hens follow and lastly the baby chicks hesitantly emerge — although one just can't wait and runs ahead.

Mary pours grain into the feeding dish and water into the trough.

Lucy wants to hold a little chick.

She has to sit on the ground so she doesn't drop it.

On the way back, they go to the lake to feed the geese.

Now Mum hurries to the garden. She has to water the plants before the sun gets too hot.

She still needs to plant some seedlings in the ground, remove the weeds and pick the first strawberries.

Mum hears a soft 'peep' and looks up at the swallow's nest.

The chicks have hatched out of their eggs and are hungry. The swallow parents will have to work very hard to catch all the flies they need to feed their young ones.

115

Dad cleans out the stable and covers the ground with fresh straw. Then he drives out to the fields on the tractor to mow the grass.

The weather will be sunny for a few days, so he can turn the hay several times for it to dry well. Then they'll make hay bales, which will be lifted into the hay loft for animal food in the winter.

Mary and Simon bring carrots and some dry bread for the rabbits.

The rabbits are allowed to run around on the grass for a while. They belong to their cousin Sonia, who is on holiday.

Lucy has managed to climb into the cart.

Simon pulls the cart around the barnyard. Lucy and her teddy have to hold tight.

Mary can't push her pram fast enough to keep up with Simon.

Oh no! The billy goat has squeezed through a hole in the fence and is running around the house. Lucy gets quite a fright and jumps into Mary's arms.

Simon tries to chase the billy goat back into the field but the goat heads straight for the garden.

Mum hears the commotion and comes out of the house. She lures the goat back into the field with a piece of bread and fastens the hole shut.

Hurray, lunch is ready.

Mum doesn't have to shout for long because everyone is very hungry. Dad is back from making hay.

Because it's such a warm sunny day, they eat out in the garden.

Everyone is looking forward to cake for dessert.

When the neighbouring children come to visit, Mum gives them a piece of cake too.

Annie really wants to see the baby kittens. Tom wants to see the piglets in the barn. It sounds so funny when they squeal!

The kittens are lying in a basket beside the kitchen stove. Annie picks up Licky, the mother cat.

Annie could play with the cats for hours. She'd love to take a kitten home with her, but they are still too small and need to drink their mother's milk. Annie hopes her parents will let her have a kitten.

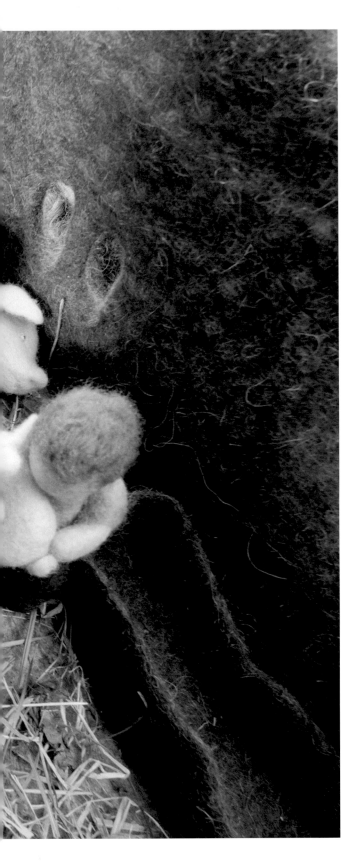

In the pigsty, the boys pick up the piglets.
But they quickly put them down again because they wriggle and squeal so much!

Tom and Simon climb on the fence. Simon calls to Max, and the horse comes trotting over.

Bravely he climbs onto his back and shouts 'giddy up', but Max just stands still and gives him a surprised look.

When Tom climbs up too, the horse tosses his mane. Both boys get a fright and quickly slide back down onto the fence.

Luckily Dad didn't see them trying to ride the horse.

He is repairing broken fences: first the cows' fence, then the sheep and goats' fence. Now the donkey is happy because he can join them in the field.

The children go to the lake. In winter, they built boats and now they want to sail them on the water.

Mum asks Mary and Annie to look after Lucy very carefully. She is not allowed to go too near the water.

The boys are already paddling barefoot. Quacking loudly, the ducks and geese swim to the other side of the lake.

Tom puts Mary's doll into a boat. Mary doesn't think it's funny at all and starts crying loudly. She pulls the doll back.

The girls start to play with a ball.

Annie doesn't catch it and splash! it lands in the water. They use sticks to fish the ball out again.

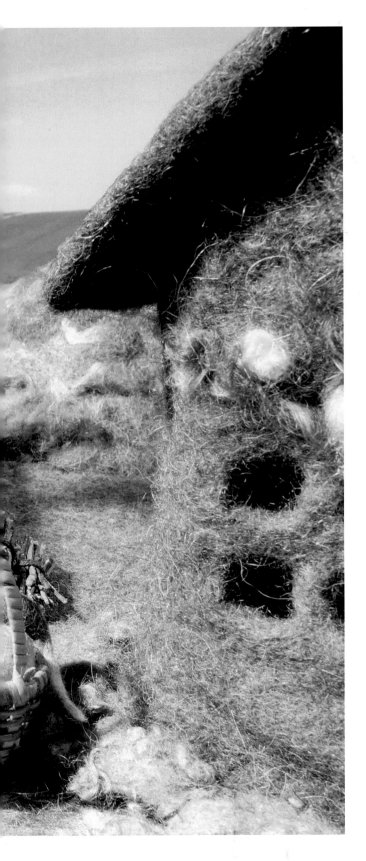

A fire is burning bright in the baking house, and the bread is waiting to be baked.

Tomorrow is market day. Mum will sell bread, jam, eggs and vegetables there. She is very busy baking and still needs to pick the vegetables and pack everything up.

She brings the children a bowl of freshly-baked cinnamon rolls. They taste wonderful.

Tom gives Sandy a piece. He can't stop stroking her; he'd really like a dog of his own.

Dad is chopping wood and stacks it beside the barn.

They need smaller twigs for the fire in the baking house, and large pieces of wood for heating the kitchen stove in the winter.

The trees were cut down last winter and Dad pulled the trunks out of the wood with Max, the strong horse.

It's late, and Annie and Tom have gone home.

Mum picks up a tired Lucy and lets the hens back into the hen house so that they are safe from the fox and pine martens at night.

The sheep and goats are quiet. They get food and fresh water in their troughs.

Mum also gives the goslings something to eat. They can already swim, even though they are very small.

Lucy doesn't want to walk any more so Mum carries her.

At night, the geese also go back into their house.

The cows need to be milked again. Dad, Mary and Simon drive the cows into the stable. Tasty food is waiting for the animals in the troughs.

While Dad milks the cows, Mary and Simon drive the pigs into the stable. They oink and grunt loudly and only stop when their trough is filled. They eat noisily.

Soon the mother pig and the piglets will join the other pigs in the field.

Before the children go into the house they feed the rabbits some dandelion leaves.

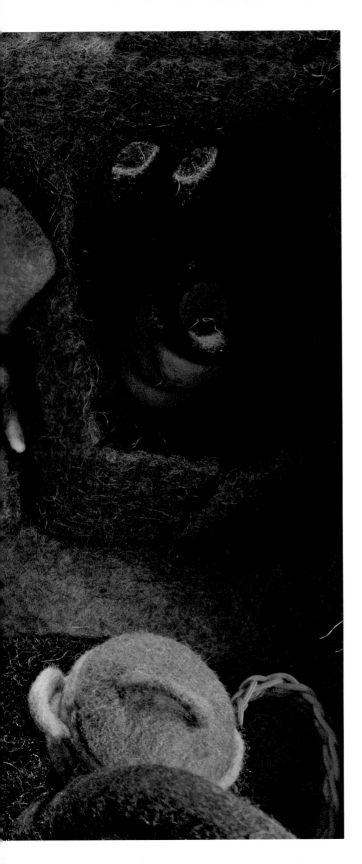

After supper, Lucy is put to bed. She is so tired from all the fresh air and sunshine that she falls asleep immediately.

The two older children are allowed to stay up. Dad reads them a story.

One of the kittens sits on Mary's lap and purrs. Sandy sits down beside Simon. He wants to be stroked. He'll get some supper too before he goes to sleep.

It's dark outside. The family are asleep.

Outside it's quiet; most of the animals are sleeping too. Sometimes a soft mooing comes from the stable. Only the cat is out, catching mice.

But someone else is also awake: the little gnome tiptoes quietly around the house and stables, keeping watch over the farm.

157

Resources

Further reading

Adolphi, Sybille, *Making Fairy Tale Scenes,* Floris Books, Edinburgh.
—*Making Flower Children,* Floris Books
—*Making More Flower Children,* Floris Books
Berger, Petra, *Feltcraft,* Floris Books, Edinburgh.
Berger, Thomas, *The Christmas Craft Book,* Floris Books, Edinburgh.
Berger, Thomas & Petra, *Crafts through the Year,* Floris Books, Edinburgh.
—, *The Gnome Craft Book,* Floris Books, Edinburgh.
Kutsch, Irmgard and Brigitte Walden, *Spring Nature Activities for Children,* Floris Books, Edinburgh.
— *Summer Nature Activities for Children,* Floris Books, Edinburgh.
— *Autumn Nature Activities for Children,* Floris Books, Edinburgh.
— *Winter Nature Activities for Chidren,* Floris Books, Edinburgh.
Kraul, Walter, *Earth, Water, Fire and Air,* Floris Books, Edinburgh.
Leeuwen, M van & J Moeskops, *The Nature Corner,* Floris Books, Edinburgh.
Müller, Brunhild, *Painting with Children,* Floris Books, Edinburgh.
Neuschütz, Karin, *Sewing Dolls,* Floris Books, Edinburgh.
Petrash, Carol, *Earthwise: Environmental Crafts and Activities with Young Children,* Floris Books, Edinburgh & Gryphon House, Maryland.
Reinckens, Sunnhild, *Making Dolls,* Floris Books, Edinburgh.
Schmidt, Dagmar & Freya Jaffke, *Magic Wool,* Floris Books, Edinburgh.
Taylor, Michael, *Finger Strings,* Floris Books, Edinburgh.
Thomas, Anne & Peter, *The Children's Party Book,* Floris Books, Edinburgh
Wolck-Gerche, Angelika, *Creative Felt,* Floris Books, Edinburgh.
— *More Magic Wool,* Floris Books, Edinburgh.
— *Papercraft,* Floris Books, Edinburgh.

Suppliers

Australia
Morning Star
www.morningstarcrafts.com.au

Winterwood Toys
www.winterwoodtoys.com.au

North America
The Waldorf Early Childhood Association of North America maintains an online list of suppliers at:
www.waldorfearlychildhood.org/sources.asp

UK
Myriad Natural Toys
www.myriadonline.co.uk

Creative Felt
Felting and Making More Toys and Gifts
Angelika Wolk-Gerche

Angelika Wolk-Gerche
ISBN 978–086315–678–6

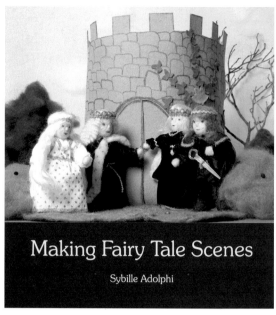

Making Fairy Tale Scenes
Sybille Adolphi

Sybille Adolphi
ISBN 978–086315–718–9

Feltcraft
Making Dolls, Gifts and Toys
Petra Berger

Petra Berger
ISBN 978–086315–720–2

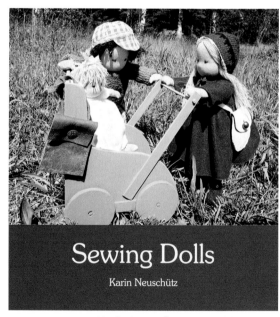

Sewing Dolls
Karin Neuschütz

Karin Neuschütz
ISBN 978–086315–719–6

www.florisbooks.co.uk